MONOPOLY
RULES

Also by Milind M. Lele

The Customer Is Key
Creating Strategic Leverage

MONOPOLY
RULES

HOW TO FIND, CAPTURE, AND CONTROL
THE MOST LUCRATIVE MARKETS
IN ANY BUSINESS

Milind M. Lele

CROWN
BUSINESS
NEW YORK

Library of Congress Cataloging-in-Publication Data
Lele, Milind M.
Monopoly rules : how to find, capture, and control the most lucrative
markets in any business / Milind Lele.— 1st ed.
1. New products—Management.   2. Product life cycle.
3. Business planning.   I. Title.
HF5415.153.L43 2005
658.5'75—dc22   2005006404

ISBN 1-4000-4972-5

10   9   8   7   6   5   4   3   2   1

FIRST EDITION

To Blair,
for all her patience during the writing of this book,
and for Hari, Gita, Girija, and Evangeline

Contents

MONOPOLY
RULES

Introduction

Conventional wisdom says that business is about producing better products at lower prices than other companies . . . about seeking sustainable advantages . . . about winning away customers from companies around the corner or around the world. Business, in short, is about *competition.*

But what if we turn conventional wisdom on its head and say that business is not about competition, but about *monopoly?* Surprise! When we do, we begin to uncover the hidden realities of business—the Monopoly Rules. The Monopoly Rules offer radically new insights about why some companies are successful, and why others fall behind; about how once-great companies often ignore opportunities in their own backyards while upstarts seize them to achieve industry dominance; and about the little-known factors that really determine the market value of a company.

In Economics 101, you probably learned that monopolies are unnatural, illegal, and rare. Wrong! Wrong! Wrong! In fact, monopolies are often natural, usually legal, and surprisingly common.

Here's a simple example. At the multiscreen cinema in Evanston, Illinois, where I go to catch the latest movies, a 32-ounce soft drink costs $3.95. Except for the price, it's the same drink as the one sold at McDonald's down the street for 99¢. It's made with the same syrup from the same supplier, served in the same kind of container, and chilled with ice made from the same city water. So why does a cola at the theater sell for four times the price of the same cola at McDonald's? Simple: The theater complex has a monopoly created by its rule that any food or drink consumed there must be purchased there. Once you choose to see a movie, if you want something to drink anytime in the next two hours, there's only one place to buy it. The theater management knows it and sets prices accordingly.

Similar monopolies exist all around us. A room at the O'Hare Hilton costs much more than a similar room in a hotel two miles away. Why? Because the Hilton offers the only lodging within walking distance of the main Chicago airport. (All other hotels are at least a mile away, requiring a cab or shuttle ride and the hassles they entail.) Business travelers who want quick access to O'Hare—for an early morning flight, for instance—have no choice but to stay at the Hilton.

Replacements for the ink-jet cartridges used by my Hewlett-Packard printer are another monopoly; and so are Harley-Davidson motorcycle accessories, Cabbage Patch Kids, and Microsoft Windows.

It's true that we usually don't think of these businesses as monopolies. To most people, the word *monopoly* means something like the old Bell telephone system, the Amtrak rail network, or a regional electric utility: a large, often regulated company that is the only source for a basic, commoditized service. But the soda fountain, the airport hotel, and the other examples we've cited are monopolies in the only sense that matters: Their customers have only one choice—to pay the price demanded, or go without.

Furthermore, as we'll show in this book, every company

that wants to enjoy lasting success and large, dependable profits *must* have a monopoly of some kind. The movie concession stand would make a lot less money if it had to charge 99¢ for a soda. In the same way, if there were three hotels across the street from the terminals at O'Hare, if using an off-brand ink-jet cartridge didn't void the warranty on my HP printer, and if any manufacturer could offer leather jackets with Harley logos, then Hilton, HP, and Harley-Davidson would all be far less profitable.

In fact, most great companies benefit from some form of monopoly. The conventional explanations offered for successful businesses are often superficial: "They have a powerful brand," "They design good products," "They've got smart management," or "They keep their costs low." Dig deeper to find out what kind of monopoly the company owns, and you get insights that are very different and ultimately more meaningful. American Express, for example, owns a great brand. But the real source of its twenty-five-year track record of success was a charge card monopoly created by regulations limiting consumer interest rates.

Dell Computer is highly efficient at manufacturing and selling personal computers. But so are many other companies. Dell's unique success is based on its ten-year monopoly—a decade when it was the *only* PC maker selling made-to-order PCs directly to corporate customers.

Like other car rental companies, Enterprise has a large fleet of well-maintained vehicles available at affordable rates. But Enterprise has become the largest car rental firm in North America because it owns a monopoly: Enterprise is the *only* major agency that caters to the market for local, non-travel-related car rentals.

This new perspective offers a very different way of thinking about a company's prospects and strategies. Most important, it focuses our attention on *ends* rather than *means*. The business leader needs to ask the fundamental question, "What kind of monopoly can our company own?" rather than concentrating on strategies for product development, finance, marketing, or sales, in hopes that they will (somehow) lead to profits. Those strategies may be valuable, but only as tools for achieving the real objective—monopoly control, which *guarantees* a company's profitability.

Recognizing the importance of monopoly is especially vital today. Just consider a few of the trends that we've seen since the turn of the new millennium. During that period, North American PC revenues have been flat; sales of music CDs have dropped 20 percent; two major airlines have filed for bankruptcy; many retailers are struggling; techies have been abandoning Silicon Valley like refugees from a disaster zone; and American manufacturers have shed jobs by the hundreds of thousands.

These trends can't be blamed solely on a bursting stock market bubble, terrorism, Internet piracy, or a prolonged recession. They are harbingers of the most far-reaching, devastating changes to the global commercial order since the Industrial Revolution. Taken together, these changes are ushering in an era I call the "New Competition."

In the New Competition, traditional sources of monopoly such as natural resources, regulation, collusion, or proprietary technologies are rapidly losing their effectiveness. Most natural resource monopolies have already been taken; governments are *de*regulating, not handing out new, regulated monopolies; and collusion is virtually impossible, as well as being illegal. Finally, proprietary technologies are leaking away, being copied, or being replaced by newer technologies faster than ever before. The New Competition is ruthlessly squeezing the profits of the old monopolies!

In this Darwinian environment, understanding monopoly is not just useful—it's essential. If you recognize your own business's monopoly and know how to exploit, nurture, and protect it, you will have a shot at earning good profits for the foreseeable future. If you don't, you'll become someone else's dinner—and probably sooner rather than later.

But there's good news, too. Even as the New Competition is destroying many old monopolies, it is creating opportunities for new ones. Many of the potential new monopolies are springing up in otherwise mature, slow-growing industries with pitifully narrow profit margins. To capitalize on these opportunities, you won't need unique products or technologies, or convention advantages based on scale, scope, or the experience curve. What you *will* need is vision and imagination: *vision* to anticipate how monopolies will emerge as customer needs and industry capabilities change, and *imagination* to determine how best to seize and hold the favored competitive positions.

This book will serve as a starter kit for developing the vision and imagination your company will need to benefit from the monopolies of tomorrow.

PART ONE

THE TRUTH ABOUT MONOPOLIES

You may think you know what a monopoly is . . . how it is created . . . how it operates . . . and the impact of monopolies on business competition. The chances are excellent, however, that most of what you think you know is wrong. In Part One, we'll explain the true nature of monopolies, show why the concept of monopoly you learned in Economics 101 is a dangerous oversimplification, and examine a host of examples, familiar and unfamiliar, that will help you understand the powerful role monopolies play in today's rapidly changing business world.

1

NO TRESPASSING

HONDA'S MINIVAN MONOPOLY

In the fall of 2002, my wife Blair and I went shopping for a minivan. Our first stop was the local Honda dealership to take a look at the top-rated Odyssey. As we were checking out the floor model, a salesman walked over.

"Hi, folks!" he said. "My name is Arnie. Can I help you?"

"I have a problem with the trunk," said Blair. "It looks awfully small. I often carry a lot of stuff, and I wouldn't know where to pack it."

Arnie smiled. "Let me show you the best feature of this van," he said. He lifted the tailgate, pulled a lever, and yanked at a strap attached to the back of the third row of seats. In seconds, the seats collapsed and folded neatly into the trunk-well, creating a huge, carpeted cargo area.

"All you have to do is push down these backseats and you can carry almost anything your heart desires. Why, just the other day I used my Odyssey to bring home a coffee table and four chairs that were on sale at Sam's Club."

Blair and I were impressed. "How soon can we take one home?" I asked.

"I'll be happy to put you on the list," Arnie replied. "There's a wait of about eight weeks right now."

"You're kidding!" I protested. "What about a used Odyssey?"

Arnie shook his head. "Don't remember the last time I saw one. People don't seem to sell their Odysseys."

Blair and I didn't relish the idea of an eight-week wait, so we thanked Arnie and drove across town to take a look at the other top-rated minivan, the Toyota Sienna.

At the Toyota dealership, a friendly saleslady named Donna showed us a shiny metallic gray Sienna. "What a beauty," she exclaimed. "Check out the carpeting, the air conditioning for the rear passengers, the automatic cruise control. And if you don't like this color, we have four others on the lot to choose from."

Blair got into the driver's seat and looked around. "Nice," she said appreciatively. "But how big is the trunk? We've got three small children and a lot of gear to carry."

"No problem. We've got one of the biggest trunks in this size van. Here, take a look."

Peering in, my wife said, "Gee, that doesn't look much bigger than the Odyssey that we just saw."

Donna was quick with an answer. "If you ever want more space, just take out the backseat and the cargo room doubles. Here, let me show you." She started tugging at various catches and levers.

"Wait a minute!" said Blair. "You mean the rear seats don't fold flat?"

"No, no!" Donna replied. "All you do is take them out of the car and you've got a nice, big cargo area."

Blair frowned. "But what do I do if I discover something I really like at Home Depot or a tag sale?" she asked. "I can't just leave the backseats on the sidewalk!"

That settled it. We signed up for a Honda Odyssey with Arnie, even though it meant waiting for nearly three months. But the whole episode left me highly intrigued. Honda had evidently found something customers wanted. They couldn't make Odysseys fast enough, and the minivans were so popular that many dealers were charging a thousand dollars or more *above* the list price. What was the matter with Toyota and the other car manufacturers? Why weren't they making minivans with seats that folded flat?

A week after our Odyssey finally arrived I learned the secret of Honda's uniqueness. When I shared the story of our car shopping experience with the participants in my marketing seminar, Bill Stowell, a product-engineering manager at a major automaker, raised his hand.

"Actually, it's not very mysterious," Bill said. "The problem is the dies that are used in making the floor pan of a minivan. They're really expensive, and they've got to be ordered eighteen months in advance, sometimes more."

"I understand," I said. "But wouldn't it be worth the money to make a product that more customers want?"

"Sure," Bill replied. "But the cost of the dies is only the

start. Changing over from one set of dies to a new set is even more expensive, since it means shutting down production for more than a week. That's why car manufacturers hold off on major changes until they're ready to introduce a new model."

"And when does that happen?"

"About once every four years."

Suddenly Honda's advantage was very obvious: Honda had introduced the Odyssey's fold-flat seats in late 1999. Given the traditional four-year product cycle, other manufacturers wouldn't come out with fold-flat rear seats until 2004 at the earliest. (Which in fact they did: Nissan's 2004 model Quest minivan had a fold-flat third row, while Ford went one better, introducing a 2004 minivan in which *both* sets of rear seats folded flat.) Until then, Honda would offer the *only* minivan with this highly desirable feature.

Honda had a monopoly! As a result, during the five-year period from 1999 to 2004, while controlling less than 10 percent of the U.S. minivan market, Honda would capture over *one-third* of the profits in this segment.

AN OWNABLE SPACE FOR A USEFUL PERIOD OF TIME

By *monopoly* I mean simply that a company or a business controls an ownable space for a useful period of time. Once again:

*A monopoly is an ownable space
for a useful period of time.*

The company owns, exclusively controls, *something*—a group of customers, a product feature, or some other desirable attribute—long enough to make some money.

This view of monopoly as "an ownable space for a useful period of time" takes us right back to the original definition: "Monopoly" is derived from the Greek word *monoplion: mono-,* meaning "only," and *plein,* meaning "to sell" or "seller." Thus, "monopoly" simply means "the only seller (of some product or service)"—somewhere, for some time. Nothing more, nothing less.

For the monopoly to be meaningful, the space must be "ownable," i.e., capable of being controlled and potentially profitable. It must have enough customers with needs that aren't being met who are willing and able to spend money to satisfy their needs. Ideally, their numbers should be growing, ensuring a steady stream of demand. The only bar in a town full of teetotalers may be capable of being controlled, but it can't be profitable and therefore isn't worth owning. By contrast, a look-alike bar on Rush Street, a popular Chicago locale, doesn't control any ownable space because it can't keep the market to itself.

You must also own the space long enough to make high, monopoly-like profits. Your "useful period of time" when you are the *only* player in this space must be long enough to give you a reasonable chance of recovering your investments, and then some. The more you have to invest to tap into those customers' requirements, the longer your useful period needs to be. If you have to build a large plant, invest $100 million in R&D, or carry out a major redesign of your products, you may need a useful period of several years. A fashion designer, on the other hand, may need just one season to recover her investments in a new design.

Honda's Odyssey minivan monopoly meets both our requirements. Honda's "ownable space"—minivan buyers with small children, the need for occasional cargo capacity, and the willingness to pay more or wait longer for it—was large. Millions of Gen-Xers were settling down, raising families, and furnishing their houses. A significant proportion of them didn't want or couldn't afford *two* large vehicles, one to carry children and the other to haul stuff. For these families, the Honda Odyssey was perfect.

Further, by design or sheer luck, Honda's decision to introduce this feature in 1999 also gave it a long useful period of time—five years. Ford, GM, and Chrysler were all introducing new models in 2000; by 1999, however, their designs were frozen. Even if they wanted to, they couldn't make a fundamental change like fold-flat rear seats to these models. If, on the other hand, Honda had introduced this feature in 1998, the other car makers could have copied it quickly, giving Honda a much smaller useful period of maybe a year.

As a result, Honda had a lucrative little monopoly in the minivan business. How lucrative? Consider that Honda sold an average of 120,000 minivans a year during this five-year period. It was able to get full price *without* spending a red cent on incentives or rebates, at a time when competitors were offering up to $2,500 off per minivan. Add in the fact that Honda Odysseys were priced approximately $1,500 higher, and you can see that Honda was making nearly $4,000 *more* per minivan than its competitors, who were earning maybe $1,000 in profits per vehicle. Multiply that by 600,000 Odysseys, and you find that Honda made over $2.4 billion in additional profits in the minivan segment.

Not bad for a row of seats that folded flat!

2

THE TWO DIMENSIONS OF MONOPOLY

AN OWNABLE SPACE . . .

Every monopoly has two dimensions: *space* and *time*. To really understand a monopoly, to know what makes it tick, you have to know what space the monopoly controls and for how long a period of time.

The ownable space can be defined and explored in a variety of ways. Is the space tangible and visible? Or is it intangible, buried inside customers' minds and needs? How did this space come about—what created it? Why did *this* company see the space and not others? How large is the space? Is it growing? How profitable is it?

Visit any large American supermarket and stroll over to the soup aisle. It's a vivid example of an ownable space you can touch and feel. You'll see an entire section with rows of red and white cans adorned with the century-old Campbell's brand. Sure, there are some blue Progresso cans and packets of soup mix on adjacent shelves. But make no mistake, the soup aisle is "Campbell" country.

There are many other companies that similarly "own"

the shelf spaces in their respective market channels. For decades, Kraft owned the dairy case in American super-markets. Consequently, the only cheese and cheese-related products that showed up in the dairy case were (surprise!) those made by Kraft. Kodak similarly owned the film case in corner photo shops and drugstores; virtually the only films these outlets sold were those made by Kodak. And as we shall see later, for a over a dozen years Dell Computer "owned" the shelf space in selling PCs direct over the tele-phone or (later on) on the Internet to corporate customers.

A geographic exclusive is another example of an ownable space. If you own the Coca-Cola bottling franchise in Man-hattan or Mongolia, you have a well-defined, profitable own-able space. While Manhattan has more customers than Mongolia, both are monopolies; in either case, if someone wants a Coke, they have to deal with the exclusive distribu-tor or go without.

A different kind of monopoly space is defined by *product or service uniqueness*. For nearly two decades, in Germany and in the United States, "economy car" meant the Volks-wagen Beetle, while in France it was the Citroën 2CV or *"Deux Chevaux."* Thanks to their unique designs, these two cars had a virtual monopoly of car buyers who valued reli-able, basic transportation.

From its founding in 1973, Federal Express owned the overnight package delivery space until 1982, when UPS came out with its Next Day Air service. Even today, people tend to say "I'll FedEx it" when referring to overnight delivery.

FedEx means "overnight," while UPS means "in a couple of days" or even longer.

Still another kind of monopoly space is defined by *price difference*. In retailing, Wal-Mart owns the low-price space, a monopoly it continually reinforces with its slogan, "Always low prices. Always." In the airline industry, Southwest Airlines owns the low-price space in the markets it serves. By contrast, Rolls-Royce owns the high-price space in the automotive marketplace.

All of the spaces we've described so far are more or less tangible. In other cases, however, the monopoly space is *intangible;* you can't see it the way you can see Campbell's Soup's space just by standing in the soup section. An intangible monopoly space is fundamentally psychological or emotional, existing in the minds and hearts of customers rather than in some physical location or even in a set of definable, concrete characteristics.

Some intangible monopoly spaces are based on *custom and tradition.* A company may own a particular customer segment mainly because of a long history of dominance that has made its brand practically synonymous with the product or service it offers. Because of Standard & Poor's long history as a purveyor of financial information, bond buyers automatically turn to the S&P ratings. On the other hand, knowledgeable mutual fund buyers want to know what Morningstar has to say about funds they are considering buying, while shoppers rely on the Consumers Union ratings when deciding which car, household appliance, or lawnmower to purchase.

Other intangible monopoly spaces are based on *intense emotional involvement.* Brands such as Apple Computer, Harley-Davidson, Porsche, or the Grateful Dead attract cult followers who have no space in their minds for any other supplier. An Apple aficionado would feel degraded by having to use a Windows-based personal computer; a member of HOG (the Harley Owners Group) will wait patiently for months to get just the right motorcycle or accessory.

In recent years, monopolies based on tangible spaces are coming under increasing pressure. They aren't generating the sales and profits they did in the past. At the same time, intangible ownable spaces are creating monopolies that are longer lasting and more profitable.

The reason is simple: If I *know* what ownable spaces you own, I can look for ways to muscle my way into them. I'll design a minivan with two rows of fold-down seats (as Ford did), I'll team up with Walgreens to create my own monopoly space for a competitive brand of photo film (as Fuji did), or I'll cut prices to entice some of your customers (as Target did). What's more, in today's intensely competitive environment, your suppliers, your channels, and your customers will actually *help* me imitate your designs, duplicate your technologies, copy your products, end-run your stores, and undercut your prices.

It's a lot harder to break into a monopoly space when its definition is intangible. How do I get inside Harley-Davidson's or Apple Computer's or Standard & Poor's ownable spaces? How do I win a place inside the heads of their customers?

What do I have to do—make better products, spend more on advertising, drop my prices, use different sales channels? Where do I even start?

THE MONOPOLY SPACE THAT
THE BIG PLAYERS OVERLOOKED

Sometimes it takes an unusual gift of insight to recognize the existence of a potential monopoly space that other companies have simply ignored.

In 1998, I landed at New York's John F. Kennedy International Airport on a bright June morning. I hadn't visited JFK in quite a while; most often, my trips to New York took me through nearby LaGuardia or Newark Airport, just over the Hudson River.

I was stunned to find the vast facility practically deserted. Almost no airplanes taking off or landing, no passengers, no hustling cabbies, no crowds of visitors—none of the hubbub and confusion I always encountered at LaGuardia and Newark. The woman at the ticketing counter was on the phone talking to her boyfriend, and the lone redcap on duty was reading the sports page of the *Daily News*.

Baffled, I approached the redcap. "What's going on? Why no traffic here at JFK?"

He shrugged. "This is typical. Once the last flights to Korea and Japan take off early in the morning, this place shuts down. It wakes up again after three o'clock, when the trans-Atlantic flights start arriving. We get a few commuter flights and maybe a charter or two. But mostly, it's dullsville!"

He went back to his paper.

Later, I mentioned the experience to my friend Brian Fischer, an expert on the airline industry. "It seems strange," he agreed, "but there's a simple explanation. JFK has always been devoted to international flights. They typically arrive and depart later in the day, between three o'clock and midnight. The only airlines with hubs at JFK were Pan Am and TWA. They used it to connect domestic passengers to their international destinations, not for domestic traffic. Of course, both Pan Am and TWA are now defunct. The other big airlines—United, American, Delta, Continental, Northwest—never did much business at JFK. And with the ability to fly passengers directly from their other hubs, they don't see any reason to."

"So JFK is practically empty half the day," I commented. "Seems weird, considering how huge it is."

Brian agreed. "Especially with LaGuardia and Newark bursting at the seams, and the airlines desperate for landing slots."

"So why hasn't some airline adopted JFK as its home?"

Brian shrugged. "It's a pain to get to—a lot farther from Midtown than LaGuardia or Newark. Cabbies hate to go there, a limo costs an arm and a leg, and the nearest subway stop is a mile and a half from any terminal.* Frankly, most

---

* Train service to JFK has been inaugurated since my conversation with Brian Fischer.

New Yorkers have forgotten JFK exists. They think of it as the place they went to pick up Grandma from Ireland, or to drop off their cousins going to England, or Israel, or India. They wouldn't *dream* of using JFK for a vacation flight to Miami."

Brian was right—at least until JetBlue was born.

Launched by entrepreneur David Neeleman in February, 2000, JetBlue Airways has converted JFK into a domestic airport where hundreds of thousands of New Yorkers catch cheap flights to Florida, the West Coast, the Caribbean, and other destinations. In less than five years, JetBlue has grown to be a major discount carrier, with sixty-eight Airbus A320s making 70,000 flights a year, over six thousand employees, and nearly $1 billion in revenues (all figures through year-end 2003). What's more, JetBlue is profitable, with operating income of more than $168 million, while most airlines are reeling under heavy, continuing losses.

From JetBlue's perspective, JFK was the perfect place to launch a discount carrier. Just look at the facts. Over ten million people live within reach of the airport—the populations of New York City, Westchester County, and half of Connecticut. These are people with above-average incomes, many of whom travel regularly to visit relatives in Florida or to vacation in the Caribbean or in California. Then throw in a huge, underutilized airport with up-to-date facilities and a management that is virtually begging someone to use it during the day. As a New Yorker might say, "What's not to like?"

As for competition, "Fuhgedaboudit!" JetBlue knew that the major airlines all had huge investments in their hubs at

LaGuardia and Newark. They were very unlikely to shift flights over to JFK to fight off a low-price player like JetBlue.

So the only *real* issue was how to get New Yorkers (and those reluctant cabbies) to make the trek to JFK. JetBlue's solution was to start with low fares (which more than make up for the cost of a longer taxi ride), then provide leather seats, music, and on-demand video at every seat. The result was a unique—and uniquely valuable—combination. As the *only* discount carrier operating from a major airport in the middle of America's single largest population base, JetBlue owned a highly profitable monopoly space.

Later in this book we'll explore the various kinds of monopoly spaces in much more detail, and consider how they can be defined, captured, exploited, defended, and overrun.

. . . FOR A USEFUL PERIOD OF TIME

Let us now turn to the second dimension of monopoly—time.

The "useful period of time"—what I will also call the "monopoly period"—can vary enormously. Some monopolies have a monopoly period as short as a few days or weeks; other monopolies may last for years or even decades. Obviously, the longer the monopoly period the better (i.e., the more valuable) the monopoly.

To understand a monopoly, you need to know the answers to a series of questions about the monopoly period. What is the source of this monopoly period—in other words, why are competitors unable to compete in this space? What's keeping them out? How long has the company owned this space? How much longer will the monopoly period last? Can the monopoly period be extended in any way?

Women's fashions are now duplicated with amazing speed, often within weeks. If a particular shade of green is hot in Milan, Paris, and New York this season, you can be sure that, well before the season ends, you will see a flood of look-alike skirts and blouses on the shelves at Banana Republic, H&M, and Zara. It's the same thing in PCs and consumer electronics. If Sony has a sleek-looking laptop that's selling well, pretty soon Toshiba, Acer, Dell, and all the others will have sleek-looking laptops with similar profiles and colors.

In these industries, brands are primarily design houses; they buy from the same suppliers and sell to the same buyers. Consequently, the moment a particular design gets a little traction—if Polo or Sony finds an ownable space with pink polo shirts or sleek laptops—Macy's and Circuit City go to Lacoste and Toshiba and say, "Why aren't *you* providing me with pink polo shirts or sleek laptops?" Lacoste and Toshiba, in turn, rush around and find out where Lauren and Sony are sourcing their pink polo shirts or sleek laptops, and either buy from the same sources or find someone who will make knockoffs quickly.

The harder it is to copy something and the greater the investment required, the longer the monopoly period lasts. As we saw, Honda's Odyssey with fold-flat seats enjoyed a monopoly period of five years because it was expensive and time-consuming for competitors to change their designs.

Similarly, Federal Express had the overnight package market to itself for ten years precisely because it took UPS a decade to realize that overnight packages were a growing market, design their own overnight delivery network, buy the planes, train the crews, and work out the myriad logistical challenges involved.

When the ownable space is protected by patents or copyrights, the monopoly period may last for decades. Chester Carlson's original patents on plain-paper copying gave Xerox a twenty-year monopoly. Walt Disney created the character of Mickey Mouse for the 1928 cartoon *Steamboat Willie,* probably not suspecting that the engaging rodent would become the foundation of an entertainment empire which, thanks to the so-called Sonny Bono Copyright Term Extension Act, will last until 2023.

Most monopolies, however, aren't protected by legal barriers like copyrights or trademarks. This means that defining the monopoly period—and finding ways to extend it—is a much more difficult challenge, as I will discuss later in this book. For now, let's reconsider the traditional definition of monopoly that you may have learned in school, and why this older notion of monopoly is no longer adequate in today's world of business.

3

ECONOMICS 101

MONOPOLY ACCORDING TO ECON 101

In business, monopoly is a four-letter word. Say "monopoly" and everyone immediately thinks, "Illegal behavior!" Monopoly means cartels like De Beers, which controls the world's diamond supply; price-fixing groups like the Organization of Petroleum Exporting Countries (OPEC); collusion, as when Sotheby's and Christie's, the two leading auction houses, colluded to keep commissions and prices stable; or other tactics to illicitly limit or eliminate competition. The only *legal* monopolies we know are regulated ones like the former Bell System, or state-owned enterprises like the Tennessee Valley Authority.

We also expect monopolies to be *large*. We instinctively think of monopolies as huge, monolithic organizations that dominate entire industries like telecommunications (the Bell system with half a million employees), postal delivery (the United States Postal Service with over 600,000 employees), railroads (the Indian Railways with over a million employees), or PC software (Microsoft, with 20,000+ employees and over $50 *billion* in cash).

This view of monopoly goes back to Economics 101, where we were taught to think of monopoly as the ultimate in imperfect competition. To quote Paul A. Samuelson's *Economics* (originally published in 1948 and still the most widely used college textbook on economics), monopoly is "the extreme case . . . of a *single* seller with practically complete monopoly power . . . [He] is the only one producing in his industry, and there is no industry producing a close substitute for his good."*

From this perspective, it's natural to assume that monopolies must be large; after all, in a monopoly a single seller dominates an entire market or industry. Monopolies must also be bad, because they reduce competition and cause consumers to pay higher prices. Consequently, anyone who has a monopoly must have done something bad to become large and eliminate competition—bought up competitors, driven them out of business, fixed prices, or formed cartels. In short, the traditional or Economics 101 view assumes that monopolies are large and illegal, unless they are government-controlled, in which case they are large and regulated.

The Economics 101 view of monopoly is rooted deep in the past. Historically, you created a monopoly by colluding with your competitors to control prices, or by being the sole

---

* Paul A. Samuelson, *Economics* (New York: McGraw-Hill, 5th edition, 1961, pp. 517–518).

owner of unique physical resources, or by controlling access to desirable markets.

In the words of Adam Smith, the eighteenth-century guru of free-market economics and author of *The Wealth of Nations,* "People of the same trade seldom meet together, but the conversation ends in a conspiracy against the public, or in some contrivance to raise prices." From time immemorial, businesses have tried to control prices and output, formally and informally. In the late nineteenth and early twentieth centuries, virtually every industry in the United States had some form of collusion or cartel controlling prices and outputs: Andrew Carnegie's U.S. Steel and related trusts controlled the steel industry, Leland Stanford's Central Pacific Railroad and other railroad trusts controlled freight rates . . . the list goes on. Through much of the twentieth century, Japanese firms linked in combines known as *zaibatsu* allocated markets among themselves. Cartels were legal in Japan until quite recently, and in Germany until 1957.

The use of political or military force to create and maintain a monopoly is also an extraordinarily common historical phenomenon. In Roman times, London was built at the only fordable spot on the lower Thames; London owned (controlled) a unique asset. In the fourteenth century, Venice became an economic power through its monopoly on salt, a highly desirable asset for preserving meat. In the fifteenth and sixteenth centuries, Spain owned all the gold mines in the New World. In 1937, the airship *Hindenburg,* filled with hydrogen, exploded in New Jersey; the reason it was filled with hydrogen was that the United States controlled all available supplies of helium and wouldn't release them to Nazi Germany.

The urge to control or own markets—often literally "captive" markets—is as old as the desire to control monopoly assets. The Roman empire was an early example of market ownership. In the eighteenth and nineteenth centuries, the British East India Company controlled India and owned the market for all British manufactured exports to India. The Dutch East India Company did the same with Indonesia and other Dutch colonies. The Boston Tea Party came about because the American colonists didn't want to be forced to buy expensive English goods, including tea.

Collusion is explicitly anticompetitive—and therefore illegal—because it forces buyers to pay more than the free-market price, sometimes much more. (Barring rigged auctions, people don't collude to keep prices *down!*) Owning unique assets or controlling access to lucrative markets virtually invited anticompetitive, i.e., illegal, behavior. If you were Venice, you didn't want somebody else selling salt in Europe, and so you built a great naval fleet to control other potential suppliers. If you were the British East India Company, you didn't want local weavers and cotton mills competing with your factories in Lancashire, and you shut them down by fair means or foul. Today, if you are De Beers, you don't want any diamonds showing up that weren't sold through De Beers. If you're Microsoft, you don't want anyone else's calendar, address book, Web browser (or whatever) to show up on Windows PCs, and you do whatever you can—including bundling your versions of those products "free" with Windows—to make sure that doesn't happen.

This historical evolution explains the Economics 101 view of monopoly as something suspect, something illegal. From this perspective, the only *legal* monopolies are the ones the government gave to you. For example, in 1716, John Law convinced the French government to give his *Compagnie des Indes* exclusive trading rights for the Mississippi River, Louisiana, China, East India, and South America, as well as a nine-year contract to be the sole royal tax collector, official mint, and an open-ended monopoly on the global tobacco trade! The Bell System was a regulated, government-approved and -supervised monopoly.

Similarly, patents and copyrights are government-granted monopolies that protect inventions, brands, or other intellectual property. Strictly speaking, these are not property rights. A patent or copyright is a contract between a sovereign power (the government) and the patent or copyright owner. The sovereign power grants a limited monopoly in exchange for some public benefit, e.g., dissemination of knowledge, innovation, public safety, and so on.

THE BELL SYSTEM: A CLASSIC ECON 101 MONOPOLY

The Bell System was a classic Economics 101 monopoly. From 1907 onward, AT&T bought up local Bell companies as well as independents. It also bought control of Western

Union, giving it tremendous pricing power in both telephone and telegraph communications. In the process, AT&T was accused of semi-illegal, if not downright illegal, methods to eliminate pesky or unwelcome competitors. Its president, Theodore N. Vail, had openly stated that there should be "one policy, one system [AT&T's] and universal service . . . [because] no collection of separate companies could give the public the service that [the] Bell . . . system could give." AT&T's management was determined to make the Bell System the "*single* seller with practically complete monopoly power."

By 1913, AT&T was a large and illegal monopoly, under increasing attack from the Department of Justice for its anti-competitive behavior and activities. This changed with the so-called Kingsbury Commitment of December 9, 1913, actually a letter from Vice President Nathan Kingsbury of AT&T to the Attorney General of the United States in response to the various Federal antitrust investigations. In that letter, AT&T agreed to sell its controlling stake in Western Union (the telegraph company), to provide long distance services to independent companies or exchanges, and to make no further acquisitions without the approval of the Interstate Commerce Commission. In 1934, the United States Government placed AT&T under the jurisdiction of the newly created Federal Communications Commission and the Bell System became a legal, regulated monopoly.

For over seventy years, from 1913 to its final breakup in 1984, the Bell System dominated telecommunications in the United States. Nine out of every ten telephones were made in the Bell System's factories, installed by Bell System installers, and serviced by Bell System maintenance staff. The Bell System connected local, long-distance, and international calls; transported data; and carried broadcast TV signals coast-to-coast and border-to-border. The Bell System built central exchanges, installed cables, launched satellites, and carried out research for new services such as PicturePhone and cellular calling. It was an enormous economic powerhouse, controlling assets valued at $149.5 billion and employing over a million workers.*

THE NEW VIEW OF MONOPOLY

Our concept of monopoly as "an ownable space for a useful period of time" is radically different. Where the Economics 101 view of monopoly is "large, illegal (or regulated), spanning an entire industry," under our definition, monopolies are "smaller, perfectly legal, and focusing on specific, often narrow, areas of markets."

Compare, for example, Honda's minivan monopoly with the Bell System. The Bell System was *huge*. Honda's minivan monopoly, by comparison, is tiny.

Initially, the Bell System was an illegal monopoly, with parent company AT&T being accused of resorting to various illicit activities to eliminate competition. Honda's minivan monopoly is completely legal. Honda didn't do anything

---

* Figures are as of December 31, 1983, just before the breakup.

illegal to reduce competition—it didn't buy up competitors, deny them service, or otherwise try to eliminate competition.

The Bell System was highly regulated, while Honda's minivan monopoly is totally unregulated (except, of course, for the standard safety requirements with which all automakers must comply). For example, Honda and its dealers can charge whatever they want: list price, above list price, below list, or whatever else they think is appropriate. The Bell System spanned the entire telecommunications industry. By contrast, Honda's minivan monopoly owns less than 10 percent of the American minivan segment; Honda is far from dominating the American automobile market.

Last but not least, the Bell System monopoly endured for seventy years, while Honda's monopoly lasted barely five!

In addition to being perfectly legal, our monopolies, unlike their Economics 101 counterparts, actually exist in competitive, often highly competitive, industries. The Bell System had no competitors; your local electric utility is the only place to get electricity; De Beers is the *only* source for diamonds; all oil-producing countries follow OPEC's pricing. Honda's Odyssey, on the other hand, competes directly with minivans from Toyota, Ford, General Motors, Chrysler, and Mazda.

What the Bell System and Honda's minivan monopoly *do* have in common is that they are both monopolies. In their respective markets (the Bell System) or ownable spaces (Honda), each company is or was the only seller. If you wanted a telephone line or wanted to call someone, you pretty much had to deal with the Bell System. If you wanted a minivan that could also be quickly changed over into a cargo carrier "without leaving the third row of seats on the sidewalk" (to use my wife's words), the Honda Odyssey was your only choice.

So please erase the Economics 101 definition of monopoly from your mind for the duration of this book, and in particular, the notion that monopoly is something antisocial, illegal, or unethical. As we shall see, monopoly is at the heart of *every* successful business—always has been, always will be—and pursuing it is not only moral but *essential* for anyone interested in creating a company with lasting value.

4

IT'S NOT ABOUT "SUSTAINABLE COMPETITIVE ADVANTAGE"

BEYOND THE BETTER MOUSETRAP

Throughout the centuries, merchants and traders have sought the Holy Grail—a business that would guarantee them a large, steady stream of income. Over time, their image of that wished-for Holy Grail has changed.

Natural resource monopolies are few and far between; after all, there are only so many locations, mines, or other *unique* natural assets. Regulatory monopolies are limited; besides, being regulated puts a ceiling on their profits. Collusion is illegal nearly everywhere; even when it is legal, as with OPEC, it's risky—your fellow price-fixers could cheat on you. Until recently OPEC's biggest problem was that many countries kept on producing more oil than they had officially agreed to produce, depressing oil prices below what OPEC members wanted.

As a result, since the late 1890s, managers have focused their attention on creating monopolies by building *something*—a product, a feature, a brand, a technology—that everyone wanted and that competitors couldn't copy because it was too difficult; too expensive; or protected by patent, copyright, or trademark. Their goal was simple—to build the proverbial "better mousetrap."

But as competition increased, a better mousetrap alone wasn't enough. Rivals began copying and even improving upon the best existing mousetraps. What was worse, imitation was more profitable than innovation: It cost less, you got your product to market faster (since copying a design is quicker and easier than creating one from scratch), and you didn't have to devote time and money to educating customers and creating demand for the product because the original inventor had already done it for you. Consequently, the focus shifted to finding a new kind of Holy Grail—something that could help a company consistently generate superior profits despite competition. In the literature of management, this grail came to be known as *sustainable competitive advantage* (SCA).

In recent years, a lot has been written by consultants and scholars about the nature of SCA. In his 1985 book, *Competitive Advantage: Creating and Sustaining Superior Performance*, the respected strategy guru Michael Porter identified two possible sources of SCA: *differentiation* and *low cost.*

Others pushed the concept much further, developing lists of specific business characteristics that could offer a sustainable competitive advantage. These included *scale* (that is, sheer size), which permits a company to make things cheaper and sell them at lower prices than its competitors; *scope,* which lets a company offer a broader, more diverse array of products than anyone else; *service quality,* which helps a company attract and retain loyal customers; *product uniqueness,* which draws customers who need or want the special attributes only your offerings can provide; *greater efficiency,* which enables a company to establish a position as the lowest-cost producer in its industry; *more extensive experience,* which facilitates more efficient learning, technological improvement, and cost reduction through the effects of the so-called experience curve; and *brand strength,* which creates a price premium and makes the branded product appear more valuable than its non-branded competition.

Throughout the highly competitive 1990s, managers worked tirelessly to identify and build up their companies' sustainable competitive advantages and to seek new sources of SCA. Some went on the acquisition trail in search of scale or scope, like the many big banks that merged to form even bigger banks, or the information/entertainment companies like AOL/Time Warner that sought SCA in the form of an unmatched array of media outlets. Others reengineered themselves repeatedly, outsourced basic functions (manufacturing to China, customer service to India), and relentlessly lowballed suppliers in search of lower costs and greater efficiency. Still others spent billions on advertising, marketing, publicity, promotions, sponsorships, and special events in hopes that the magic elixir of brand strength might help them stand out from the competition.

THE "GOOD-TASTING-CUP-OF-COFFEE" MONOPOLY

There's nothing wrong with most of the tactical steps suggested by the promoters of SCA. Trimming costs? Improving quality? Sprucing up your brand image? All are fine ideas that may even boost your profit margins by a point or two. *But none of these highly touted paths to sustainable competitive advantage offers a guarantee of profitability. Only monopoly can do that.*

Furthermore, although the concept of SCA is supposed to offer an all-embracing explanation of business success, it actually does very little to shed light on some of the most startling success stories of the last dozen years.

Consider, for example, the well-known saga of Starbucks Coffee. Since 1971, Starbucks has grown from a single store in Seattle's Pike Place Market to a chain of more than eight thousand cafes throughout the United States and in thirty-one overseas markets. With over $4 billion in sales (fiscal 2003), Starbucks has made the cup of coffee into big business while it created a minor revolution in tastes and lifestyles.

So far, so familiar. The surprise is here: *Starbucks achieved its amazing success without the help of any of the traditional sustainable competitive advantages.*

For its first decade or more, Starbucks had no advantage of scale: It wasn't big enough to buy coffee cheaper than Nestlé, General Foods, or any other large company.

It had no truly unique products: Cappuccinos, lattes, and

iced coffees, not to mention regular and decaffeinated coffee, have all been around for a long time.

It had no experience curve advantage: The business of brewing and serving coffee dates back at least to the London coffeehouses of the 1700s. In such a mature industry, Starbucks had no hidden expertise to draw on.

It had no brand advantage: For many years, few people had heard of Starbucks, and to this day the company doesn't advertise heavily.

And Starbucks was definitely not the low-cost producer: Most towns had plenty of diners, coffee shops, and cafeterias that sold a cup of java for a third of the cost of a typical Starbucks brew.

So, why did Starbucks succeed?

In search of an answer, I visited my friend Sam Hill, who has analyzed the Starbucks phenomenon in great detail. His curiosity is partly personal—Sam likes coffee—and partly professional: As a marketing consultant, former vice-chairman of a major advertising agency, and author of several books on branding and marketing strategy, Sam simply *had* to know.

I asked Sam, "Today, when you say 'coffee,' most people will say, 'Starbucks.' But a few years ago, people would have mentioned Maxwell House, Folgers, Nescafé, or one of the other supermarket brands. What happened?"

"Real simple," said Sam. "Supermarket coffee tastes lousy. No matter what you do with it—percolate it, brew it with a filter, use an espresso machine—it stinks. When people try Starbucks and find out what coffee could—and should—taste like, it's like a giant lightbulb goes on inside their heads: 'So coffee doesn't have to taste awful? Wow!' That's all it takes to make people switch."

"I don't get it," I said. "If it's just a matter of great coffee, why did it take so long for somebody like Starbucks to make it available?"

"Let me give you a little history," Sam replied. "Before World War II, Americans drank some of the best coffee in the world. And they drank more coffee per capita than people in any other country. But after World War II, the quality of American coffee sank like a stone. And so did coffee consumption.

"It all goes back to the coffee bean. The original coffee bean was from a tree with the botanical name *Coffea arabica.* Coffee made from arabica beans is very flavorful and mild. If you've had Turkish coffee, made the right way, you'll know what I mean.

"Unfortunately, arabica is expensive to grow and is subject to devastating attacks from a fungus that causes wild swings in production and prices. In the late 1800s, Brazil started to produce a different strain of coffee, resistant to this fungus, that grows on a tree known as *Coffea canephora.* The beans themselves, however, are usually called *robusta.* These beans grow faster, survive changes in weather, and have other advantages in cultivation. There's only one problem: Coffee made from robusta beans tastes awful.

"But since both consumers and roasters wanted stable, low coffee prices, coffee makers started adding a little robusta to their blends. At first it was just a little, to help stabilize the prices, but once coffee marketers realized how much cheaper robusta was in comparison to arabica, greed took over. By the mid-1950s, almost all the coffee sold in supermarkets was 100 percent robusta."

"So that's how American coffee got to be so bad—before Starbucks," I said.

"That's it," Sam said. "The gaping hole in the market left by the major brands was ready to be filled by a company that would offer truly delicious coffee. Starbucks was that company."

"Is that all there is to the story?"

"Not quite," Sam said. "Starbucks caught on for several additional reasons. First, fortuitously or otherwise, their timing was excellent. American coffee drinkers were finally sick and tired of the terrible stuff they were getting and were ready—make that *eager*—for something better. And with millions of American families turning into two-earner households, there were plenty of busy working folks, men and women who needed a quick pick-me-up in the morning but didn't necessarily have time to brew it at home. They were willing to spend a buck or two for a delicious treat on their way to the office.

"Starbucks also made some very smart business decisions. By not franchising Starbucks outlets, the company made certain that the coffee would taste good *consistently*. Very important. As the familiar Starbucks logo began to pop up on more and more street corners, fans recommended the coffee to their friends, knowing it would always be delicious,

unlike the wildly varying quality of coffee from the traditional diner or cafeteria.

"Starbucks was also smart about the way they expanded
nationwide. Having designed their format, Starbucks got out
there first, and *fast*. The obvious move would have been to expand gradually out of Seattle, maybe opening up some shops
in the suburbs, then testing out Portland or Walla Walla or
some other locations in the Northwest. Instead, Howard
Schultz gambled on a leap to Chicago, two thousand miles
away. It worked big time, even though he opened in Chicago
in October 1987, the month the Dow dropped 500 points!

"From Chicago, Starbucks jumped to Los Angeles, up
the coast to San Francisco, and then cross-country to Boston.
Those few cities—all of them hip, urban enclaves with lots of
students, artists, and what were then called yuppies—became
centers of a Starbucks cult. People would look envious when
you said you had a Starbucks outlet in your neighborhood,
and when Starbucks finally came to your town, it was big
news. In a few short years, Starbucks became a national
phenomenon."

So Starbucks had none of the conventional sustainable competitive advantages. What did it have? It had a
monopoly—the good-tasting-cup-of-coffee monopoly. Consequently, Starbucks made lots of money, the kinds of unusual
profits that professors of Economics 101 call "monopoly
rents." Folgers, Maxwell House, and Nestlé, on the other
hand, had strong brands but no monopoly—no profitable,
ownable space. As a result, they were battling to sell coffee at
$4.50 a pound, while Starbucks, in effect, was selling it at

$45 a pound—and couldn't open stores fast enough to satisfy its eager customers.

SOUTHWEST AIRLINES: THE REAL STORY

For another example, let's consider another of the great business success stories of the past generation—Southwest Airlines.

Ask any group of executives why Southwest Airlines has remained on top for so many years in the intensely competitive airline industry, and you'll hear a chorus of answers that hark back to the theory of SCA.

"Southwest Airlines has an incredible sustainable competitive advantage as *the* low-cost producer in the United States airline industry. It costs them 7.2¢ to fly a passenger one mile—30 percent lower than American's cost of 11.3¢. That's why they can fly you the 225 miles from Chicago to Detroit for $39 and still make a $22 profit."

"They save money by using the same kind of planes everywhere. They don't have to train pilots or crews on different types of aircraft or argue with their workers about assignment rules or differential pay scales for varying equipment."

"They fly into secondary airports that have lower landing fees."

"They have the highest aircraft utilization rates of any domestic airline. They turn planes around between flights in just fifteen minutes, then keep those planes in the air longer, working harder, than any other airline."

"Their fare schedules are very simple so they don't spend a lot of time and money on promoting low-fare specials."

"Southwest's people work harder, and do multiple tasks. Reservation agents will help load and unload luggage. Cabin crews pitch in to clean the interiors."

"They don't serve meals on their flights—just toss you a bag of peanuts."

"They have no unions." (This last one is not true. Surprisingly, Southwest Airlines actually has the *highest* percentage of unionized employees in the airline industry.)

All these explanations add up to one big point: Southwest Airlines is the poster child for the importance and value of being the low-cost producer—the classic SCA.

There's only one problem with this theory: It's not true. In reality, Southwest Airlines has been successful when—and only when—it had a monopoly: a monopoly on cheap airline seats.

Let's say you want to travel from Chicago to Washington, D.C. You can take United or American from O'Hare to National Airport and pay $600-plus, roundtrip. Or you can travel to Midway (Chicago's alternative airport, located on the city's south side), take Southwest Airlines to Baltimore for $199 and cab it to D.C.. You'll save over $400, even after paying for two additional cab fares.

Is this an attractive trade-off? Not for everyone. Suppose you're a business traveler. If you live on the north side of Chicago (or in the northern suburbs, as I do), traveling down to Midway is a pretty big hassle. You're more likely to fly out of O'Hare on United or American and let your corporate travel office pay a little extra for the convenience.

But for the budget traveler—the student, the retiree on a fixed income, or the vacation planner trying to squeeze the most fun out of a small holiday nest egg—it's a different story. Your only alternatives are a Greyhound bus or an Amtrak train, neither of which is appealing. Either trip will entail a day and a half in a stiff, uncomfortable seat, and Amtrak will be nearly as expensive as an airplane ticket. The best choice, by far, is Southwest.

Apply this story to all of Southwest's routes, and you have the secret of the company's success. From its start in 1971, Southwest worked to create and protect an exclusive lock on price-conscious travelers within its chosen markets. This cheap seat monopoly is the *real* key to Southwest's success. All the specific strategies—rapid turnaround time, flexible work rules, the single aircraft style, bags of peanuts—are *means* used to exploit this monopoly. But without the monopoly, Southwest would be just a low-cost player in a ruthlessly competitive industry. If it got into a price war, it might bleed less than the other guy, but it would still bleed.

Southwest learned this lesson in 1994, when United Airlines launched Shuttle by United in California. United's goal was simple: to cut into Southwest's traffic in the lucrative West Coast markets. For two years, Southwest and United fought toe-to-toe across the state, but especially on the highly traveled San Francisco–to–Los Angeles route. Neither side was willing to give an inch, and both lost money.

Southwest didn't start to make money on the West Coast again until it shifted the game in such a way as to re-create its monopoly. Here's what happened: Instead of flying from San Francisco to Los Angeles International (LAX), Southwest started flying out of Oakland. Leisure and budget travelers who lived in the San Francisco area didn't mind—they just drove across the Bay Bridge and hopped on the plane in Oakland. But business flyers found it very inconvenient, especially those who were connecting from other airlines. There was no way they were going to get off a plane in San Francisco, take a cab across the Bay to Oakland, and *then* grab the Southwest flight to LAX!

So business travelers shifted en masse to United, which accordingly raised its rates. United knew that flyers equipped with expense accounts would be willing to spend a couple of hundred dollars more to save time and aggravation on their next business trip. But the budget travelers stuck with Southwest. Relieved of the competitive pressure from United, Southwest was able to raise its fares back to a profitable level—while remaining significantly lower than any competing carrier. Monopoly restored, Southwest thrived again.

So being a low-cost producer is not in itself a guarantee of profitable, let alone sustained, success—not even for a paragon of cost control like Southwest. *Only monopoly offers that guarantee.*

Perhaps you're wondering whether Starbucks and Southwest are anomalies—weird exceptions that don't really shatter the general rule that sustainable competitive advantage is the key to success.

The answer is no. In industry after industry, I've found examples of *highly* successful companies with *no* sustainable competitive advantages. Some of these companies are relatively small, even obscure: Standard Brands' Egg Beaters, Iams (pet food), Whole Foods Market (groceries), Enterprise Rent-A-Car (car-rental). Others are large and widely known: CNN, Nokia, Wal-Mart, Federal Express, Vanguard mutual funds, and Dell Computer.

This diverse group of companies has several things in common. First and foremost, *sustainable competitive advantage does not explain their success.* Even today, some of these companies have none of the commonly accepted sources of sustainable competitive advantage. They have no economies of scale or scope, no major cost advantages, no benefits from learning curves, no particularly strong brands or unique products. Others developed these advantages *after* becoming highly successful; for example, after achieving significant size, they were able to buy raw materials at lower prices and thereby reduce their overall costs. But the SCAs were not instrumental in their attaining success in the first place.

Nokia, for example, is often used as the exemplar of unique product differentiation in the cellular telephone industry. Yet Nokia was originally a little-known paper maker; it licensed much of its key technology from Motorola; and, in any case, every cellular telephone must have a standard set of features and functions. As a result, Nokia started out with no brand, no scale, and no unique product. How then did Nokia go from entrant to number one in the North American cell phone market?

Wal-Mart provides another fascinating example. Business gurus like to point to Wal-Mart's SCAs: its unequalled logistical systems, its enormous scale, its ultra-low cost structure. But when Pankaj Ghemawat, a leading academic researcher on sustainable advantage, studied how Wal-Mart achieved its status as the world's leading retailer, he noticed that the chain originally focused on small-town locations.* The key insight follows: "[M]ost of these small towns could not support two discounters, so once Wal-Mart made a long-lived, largely unrecoverable investment to service such a town, it gained *a local monopoly*" (italics mine). Ghemawat goes on to explain that these local monopolies financed Wal-Mart's investments in large regional distribution centers, and other factors that made Wal-Mart a low-cost producer.

In other words, Wal-Mart's monopoly came first; its sustainable advantage came later. Wal-Mart's SCAs helped improve its profits, but they didn't create the profits in the first place.

Second, *most of these companies have succeeded in mature, highly competitive industries.* Think about it: airlines, grocery retailing, mutual funds . . . none of these industries is exactly wide-open and growing at a double-digit rate. Monopoly can enable companies to succeed in inhospitable business regions where SCAs yield few benefits.

Third, *these companies are not one-year wonders.*

* Pankaj Ghemawat, "Sustainable Advantage," *Harvard Business Review,* Sept.–Oct. 1986, p. 54.

Every one of these firms has been growing for a long time—five, ten, twenty, even thirty years. They have all been consistently profitable, even in industries with terrible economics. For example, Southwest Airlines, unique among air carriers, has never posted an annual loss, not even after the industry was devastated by the terrorist attacks of September 11, 2001.

Fourth, *these companies have thrived even as competitors with demonstrable SCAs have struggled or even disappeared.* Enterprise Rent-A-Car has been consistently profitable, while the profits of Hertz and Avis have oscillated wildly despite powerful brand advantages. Iams has outperformed Ralston Purina and all the other major pet food brands. Nokia bested Motorola despite the latter's advantages in technology, brand, and scope. Dell Computer is growing at double-digit rates, while Compaq, DEC, and NCR—all companies that once boasted strong brands, huge customer bases, and/or technological advantages—are long gone.

Considering this list, I began to ask myself, "Does sustainable competitive advantage really matter? Or is it the Anna Kournikova of strategy—lots of endorsements, but no tennis championships?"

Here's my answer: *Sustainable competitive advantage is neither necessary nor sufficient to ensure high profits.* All SCA can guarantee is that your company will be superior to its competitors in one or more specific areas. That's it! It's possible that this will translate into higher profits, either because you can charge more, produce goods for less, make a better product, or in some other way. Possible, but far from guaranteed.

The guarantee you're looking for comes from owning a monopoly. You can make a lot of money with no SCA *if* you own a monopoly. But you can't make a lot of money (at least not consistently) if you have an SCA but *no* monopoly.

Here's an example. Everyone agrees that a respected, well-known brand can be a great competitive advantage. A strong brand operating in a monopoly space is an unstoppable profit dynamo. But when the monopoly space vanishes, all you have is an expensive marketing campaign and lackluster profits. Forty years ago, Cadillac was a great brand-based monopoly—it owned the prestige car space in North America, and as a result it earned tremendous (monopoly) profits. Today, with Mercedes-Benz, BMW, Lexus, Infiniti, and other invaders having captured much of the prestige car space, Cadillac is saddled with the high costs of supporting the famous name—but with no monopoly profits for show for it.

Here's another way to think about sustainable competitive advantage: *The traditional SCA—a unique product, a strong brand, large scale, low costs—is only a useful means. Monopoly is the end.*

Intuitively, business people have always understood this. Over time, however, we've forgotten that the purpose of the better mousetrap is to catch customers—not mice. We've fallen victim to the better mousetrap fallacy, the belief that a better mousetrap, in and of itself, will make the world beat a path to our door. It won't—only a monopoly can have that effect. As a result, we focus on the wrong issue. We keep asking, "How can we beat the existing players at what they're doing?" Instead, we should be asking, "Where can we create a monopoly space in this market? How? And for how long?"

To paraphrase the famous Clinton campaign motto, we need to keep reminding ourselves, "It's the *monopoly,* stupid!"

5

MONOPOLY FLAVORS

LIPITOR, COKE, AND THE SUPER BOWL

In 1986, working in a lab in Ann Arbor, Michigan, an organic chemist named Bruce Roth developed a method for synthesizing a compound called atorvastatin calcium. It's a powerful inhibitor of the enzyme HMG-CoA reductase, which affects the body's production of the worrisome substance known as cholesterol. Ten years later, after extensive clinical trials, the company Roth worked for—the pharmaceutical giant Pfizer—brought to market its patented version of the compound, known by the trade name Lipitor. Today, tens of millions of patients around the world take daily doses of Lipitor in hopes of reducing their cholesterol and, in turn, their chances of suffering a heart attack.

In pharmaceutical industry terms, Lipitor is one of the world's blockbuster drugs. It has a dominant 43 percent share of the worldwide market for the broad class of drugs known as statins; it boasts annual sales revenues exceeding $10 billion, and earns humongous profits for Pfizer under patent protection that will continue until at least 2009.

Back in May 1886, an Atlanta pharmacist named John S. Pemberton concocted a sweet, fizzy drink containing extract from the leaves of the coca plant along with syrup from the cola nut. He believed it would be a suitable tonic for sufferers from nervous disorders. Pemberton's accountant, Frank Robinson, suggested calling it Coca-Cola and penned the name in a flowing script design that would ultimately become familiar the world over.

Soon Coca-Cola (minus the coca extract) became popular among a far wider audience than nervous sufferers. The astute brand managers of the Coca-Cola Company staked out a position for their drink as "a delightful, palatable, healthful beverage" that has remained essentially unchanged to this day. They created packaging breakthroughs like the famous contour bottle (1915) and reinforced the drink's appeal through one of business's first brand image standardization programs (1931). Today, widely regarded as the most powerful brand in the world, Coke is sold in bottles, cans, and over the counter to countless millions of consumers in more than 200 countries.

Once a year on a late winter Sunday, scores of millions of spectators around the world turn on their televisions to watch an American football game—the Super Bowl. Those three and a half hours of gridiron action—together with countless hours of interviews, previews, and special entertainment before and after the game—generate a gusher of money that Midas himself would have envied. For the NFL, every Super Bowl generates hundreds of millions in revenue from television rights, ticket sales, merchandise tie-ins, corporate sponsorship, and a host of other sources, while the network broadcasting the game rakes in nearly a billion dollars from advertisers eager to hawk their products and services to an audience in excess of 130 million people in the United States and millions more overseas. In fact, nine of the fifteen highest-rated TV shows in history have been Super Bowl games.

What do Lipitor, Coke, and the Super Bowl have in common? All three, of course, are monopolies, businesses that control an ownable space for a useful period of time and thereby generate huge profits for their owners.

But in every other way, they are completely different. Lipitor is a prescription drug with a monopoly protected by government-issued patents. Coca-Cola is a beverage that competes for market share with similar drinks, from Pepsi-Cola to your local supermarket's no-name cola; Coke's real monopoly is its powerful brand, which is protected by copyrights and trademarks. The Super Bowl is a sports-driven event; its monopoly is based on the fact that the National Football League controls the performance and broadcasting of professional games of American-style football, an increasingly popular sport that is uniquely suited for presentation on television.

LARGE AND LONG VS. SHORT AND SMALL

As these examples illustrate, monopolies come in different flavors. Understanding the flavor of your monopoly is essential!

If you don't know what kind of monopoly you have, how can you judge how valuable it is, how long it will last, or how best to protect and exploit it? At best, you will be fumbling in the dark, hoping to find strategies that will work. More likely, you will be caught by surprise when competitors invade and your monopoly disintegrates.

One way of classifying monopolies is by the size of their ownable space and the length of their monopoly period. At one extreme, the space may be small, with a limited number of customers and a duration of just a few days. At the other extreme, the ownable space could be huge, spanning continents, including millions of customers, and lasting for years or decades.

The 2008 Summer Olympic Games will be held in Beijing. If you happen to own a well-appointed house or apartment located within a convenient distance of the main Olympic venues in Beijing, you own a monopoly. Hundreds of ticketholders and media members will be interested in bidding on the right to occupy those rooms for three weeks in 2008. But by comparison with many other monopolies, it's a small monopoly with a short monopoly period. You'll have to earn your profits—literally "monopoly rents," in this case—while the games are in town; the day after the closing ceremony, your apartment's value will drop back to normal.

Ever read the Bluffton, Indiana, *News-Banner?* Unless you're one of the 9,536 residents of this town northeast of Indianapolis, the answer is almost certainly no. But the local newspaper has a definite monopoly. If you live in Bluffton, the *News-Banner* is your sole source for finding out what's happening in your neighborhood, who's moving in, who's leaving, what the city council's thinking about, and which merchants are having sales. If you're a car dealer, hardware store, or grocery store in or around Bluffton, the *News-Banner* is the only reliable way to reach your customers. The paper has a small ownable space, but its monopoly period is fifty years and counting.

(Legendary investor Warren Buffett is well aware of the monopoly power wielded by the newspaper in a particular community. That's why, years ago, he purchased shares of the company that publishes the *Washington Post*. In Buffett's terminology, the *Post* owns the "franchise" for readers who *must* know the latest news and gossip about the federal government—who's in, who's out, and how power is shifting around town. That includes lobbyists, party activists, political operatives and consultants, and would-be opinion shapers— many thousands of people across America who *need* a subscription to the *Washington Post*. Of course, Buffett's "franchise" is just another word for monopoly.)

Sporting events like the Super Bowl, soccer's World Cup, the Wimbledon tennis championship, and the Olympic Games are, in a sense, the opposite of the Bluffton *News-Banner*: They own world-sized spaces, but their monopoly period is short. For a day, a week, or a fortnight, fans everywhere are intensely interested in the events. But when the event is over, the monopoly disappears, until it is resurrected next year or four years hence.

CLEAR VS. FUZZY

A second way of categorizing monopolies is as *clear* or *fuzzy*, depending on whether their ownable spaces and monopoly periods are well-defined or blurry, with gray areas and uncertainty about exactly where they begin and end.

If your monopoly is based on a patent, trademark, or copyright, your monopoly period is defined by law. Except in the rare case where a company has the clout to effect a *change* in the law to protect its property (as Disney did, through effective lobbying to extend copyright protection when Mickey Mouse was threatened), you know exactly when the clock will run out on your monopoly. On the other hand, the size of your ownable space may be quite fuzzy, especially if you are a first-time inventor, author, or creator; it's very hard to predict how many customers are included in your market space or how much revenue it will generate.

Conversely, the Bell System's ownable space was clearly defined: If you lived anywhere in the United States, you were part of the Bell System's monopoly (except for a tiny handful of areas controlled by GTE or other non-Bell telephone monopolies). However, its monopoly period was fuzzy, since it was ultimately dependent on the goodwill of the Federal Communications Commission. Campbell's Soup's monopoly space is similarly well defined: The company dominates every supermarket soup aisle in the United States. But its monopoly period is fuzzy: We have no idea when someone might come along and grab a big chunk of Campbell's space.

In the case of Lipitor, both the ownable space and the monopoly period are well defined. Lipitor's ownable space is all those adults with high cholesterol who respond to statins; thanks to public health statistics, we can measure fairly accurately how large this space is. Lipitor's monopoly period is defined by the fact that its main patents expire in 2009, at which point generic drug makers can enter the market with their own versions of atorvastatin.

Then there's Starbucks. In this case, both the ownable space and the monopoly period are fuzzy. The space includes all those coffee drinkers who are willing to pay more for a good-tasting cup of coffee. But how do we quantify that audience? It varies by geography (right down to specific store location) and fluctuates daily, weekly, and monthly as individual incomes, economic conditions, and tastes in beverages change. Starbucks' monopoly period is equally fuzzy. We have no clear idea when—or even whether—Starbucks will face an effective national competitor offering a comparable product in most of Starbucks' neighborhoods.

ASSETS VS. SITUATIONS

Finally, we can classify monopolies by examining their sources, their root causes. These break down into two broad categories.

First, there are what we call *asset monopolies.* As the name implies, these are based on tangible assets—limited natural resources, unique products, breakthrough technologies, licenses, patents, trademarks, copyrights, or other valuable goods controlled by a single company.

The De Beers diamond cartel, founded by South African mining magnate Sir Ernest Oppenheimer in 1934, owns a virtually complete monopoly over the world's diamond supply. Either directly or through associated companies, De Beers buys all the rough diamonds produced by mines in Africa, Russia, Australia, and elsewhere, values them and sells them to a limited number of "sightholders," who then distribute them to diamond cutters, jewelers, and retailers around the world. This is a classic asset monopoly, based on one company's absolute control over the production and distribution of a highly valued product.

It's easy to think of other examples of asset monopolies, many of them based on control of unique products. As we've seen, Honda had an asset monopoly in the fold-flat third seat for its Odyssey minivan. Inchcape had an asset monopoly as the exclusive distributor of Toyotas in the United Kingdom, Hong Kong, and elsewhere in Asia. In the United States, Scholastic Books has an asset monopoly as the exclusive publisher of the Harry Potter fantasy novels written by J. K. Rowling. In each of these cases, we can point to a specific, tangible asset that the company owns or controls.

A special subcategory of asset monopolies are what we call *brand monopolies*. These are situations in which a company has developed such a powerful brand image that it is able to command a significant price premium (a "monopoly rent") even when selling a product that is otherwise indistinguishable from the products offered by competitors.

Absolut Vodka offers a vivid illustration of the power of a brand monopoly. By definition, vodka is a colorless, odorless, almost flavorless liquor of neutral spirits distilled from mash. It's prized for making cocktails precisely because it doesn't fight the flavor of orange juice, tonic, vermouth, or any other mixer. Therefore, any difference in price between the cheapest available vodka and the most costly can only be attributed to brand image—the intangible cluster of emotions, attitudes, and ideas that adheres to a product and changes its perceived value in the mind of a consumer.

In the case of Absolut, the process by which brand value was created is well known. Starting in 1980, Absolut was promoted in upscale magazines through a unique series of clever, sophisticated, and visually stunning advertisements that punned on the product's brand name in scores of varied ways. These ads, produced by the TBWA\Chiat\Day agency, vaulted Absolut to the leading position among vodkas. For a time, Absolut owned the monopoly space defined as "vodka for urban sophisticates." Thousands of vodka drinkers would have felt embarrassed to be caught ordering anything other than Absolut—even though almost none of them could have distinguished their brand from Smirnoff or Gilbey's in a blind taste test.

The line between a brand monopoly and a monopoly based on a product or other tangible asset isn't always crystal clear. Is Coca-Cola a brand monopoly or a product-based monopoly? Perhaps a little of both. The appeal of the Coke brand is undeniable. But Coke also is arguably a "unique product," thanks to its famous secret formula (known only to a handful of company executives) and its taste, which is at least slightly different from that of Pepsi and other cola drinks.

Disney is another example. Researchers found that an animated cartoon from a different movie studio earned significantly higher audience ratings when the Disney logo was fraudulently affixed to it. Thus, the Disney brand carries a special value that makes it unique among purveyors of family entertainment. But Disney's value also derives from a genuinely unique array of products, from copyrighted characters to classic movies, songs, and TV shows.

Perhaps the lesson taught by companies like Coke and Disney is the enormous profit-making power generated by a unique product or other tangible asset *in combination with* a carefully crafted, lovingly nurtured brand name—in effect, two monopolies in one.

THE REPLACEMENT CAR MONOPOLY

The second major category of monopoly—and potentially the more interesting—is what we call a *situational monopoly*. It exists when a company is the only supplier of a certain product or service to customers in a particular combination of markets, needs, times, and positions. The company enjoys its monopoly not by virtue of having any unique products to offer or an especially appealing brand; instead, the monopoly exists simply because the company is the only one operating with the right product or service, in the right place, at the right time.

For an example, consider one of today's least-recognized monopolies, a company that definitely operates within a highly competitive industry: Enterprise Rent-A-Car.

I was discussing my ideas about monopoly with two friends I'll call Peter and Dave. Peter was former president and chief operating officer of one of the largest consumer packaged goods firms, and Dave was head of the strategy practice at a large consulting firm.

"If the monopolies you're describing don't have any sustainable competitive advantages, what creates the monopoly?" asked Dave.

"It's a combination of unmet needs, competitor inertia, and an industry dynamic that makes existing players ignore the business opportunity," I replied.

"Are you saying a new monopoly is accidental?" Peter asked.

"That's one way of putting it," I replied. "Typically, these new monopoly opportunities are created because incumbents are oblivious to them."

"Sounds too good to be true," said Dave. "Give us an example."

"Okay," I said. "Why do you think Enterprise Rent-A-Car is successful? Do they have a unique source of cars?"

"No," said Peter. "They buy fleets of cars from General Motors or Ford, just like Hertz, Avis, National, and all the other rental car companies."

"Are their prices any lower than the others?"

"Not particularly," replied Dave. "We used them when my wife's car was in the shop, and they cost about what I pay for Avis or Hertz on the road."

"Do they advertise like Hertz and Avis do? Ever see O. J. Simpson running through airports in an Enterprise ad?"

Peter had to think hard to remember a single ad for Enterprise. Finally, he thought of one: "I caught one of their ads on TV two years ago. It was sort of goofy—showed a car wrapped in brown paper. What kind of ad is that?"

"So what's unique about them?" I asked.

"They pick you up and drop you off," said Dave. "At least that's what they did when my wife rented from them. They took Sally over to their neighborhood office in the car she was going to rent, and when Sally turned it in they brought her right back."

"That's nice," interrupted Peter. "But how does that give them a monopoly? They sound to me like a nice little niche business, focused on renting to people whose cars are in the shop for repairs."

"Well, Peter," I replied with a smile. "What would you say if I told you that Enterprise is the largest car rental company in North America?"

"You're kidding," he replied.

"No, I'm not. Enterprise is bigger than Hertz, Avis, National, Budget, Alamo, or any of the others. They are a $6 billion company with 600,000 vehicles in their fleet, more than 50,000 employees, and over 4,800 locations. What's more, they're profitable and have always been profitable, which is more than you can say about the rest of the rental car crowd."

"Wow!" said Peter and Dave, simultaneously.

"Okay, so they're big. But what's their monopoly?" Peter insisted.

I turned to Dave. "What were Sally's rental choices when her car was in the shop?"

"Gee, I don't really know," said Dave. "The service manager at the dealership sent her to Enterprise. I don't think she even looked at anybody else."

"Why not?" I pressed. "After all, you're a Hertz #1 Club Gold member, aren't you? Why didn't you use your membership to get her a replacement?"

"Well, for one thing," Bruce replied, "the nearest Hertz outlet is at the airport, ten miles away from where we live. So Sally would've had to take a taxi to the Hertz place. When you add that in to the cost of the rental, Hertz would've been too expensive and too much hassle."

"So there were no other choices?" I asked.

"I guess not," said Bruce. "Enterprise pretty much had a monopoly on the replacement car for Sally."

Quite a monopoly—especially for a company with no discernible SCA.

THE BOTTOM LINE

Enterprise's monopoly grows out of its unique situation: It was, and is, *the* provider of rental cars for nonvacationers who must temporarily replace their own vehicles. Sounds boring, and in a way it is. If there were half a dozen companies doing exactly the same thing as Enterprise, it would probably be a lousy business. But since Enterprise is the only company operating in exactly this space, it is extraordinarily profitable.

Asset monopolies (including brand monopolies) are relatively easy to see and understand. They are based on things we can touch, feel, or relate to on an emotional level—a unique product, an admired brand. Situational monopolies are more complicated and subtle. But in today's ultracompetitive environment, there are more opportunities to find and exploit situational monopolies than asset monopolies. What's more, the very factors that make it difficult to spot a situational monopoly—its complexity and subtlety—will also help to shield it from attack by competitors.

Let's conclude this chapter on the flavors of monopolies by underscoring the point with which we began: Understanding the precise nature of the monopoly you own (or seek to create) is crucially important. If you don't, you're likely to commit a strategic misstep that may lead to the destruction of your monopoly and, perhaps, of your company.

In the mid-1990s, NCR enjoyed a monopoly in data warehousing. Unfortunately, the company's management misunderstood the source of that monopoly. They thought they owned an asset monopoly based on their superior technology. In actuality, it was largely a situational monopoly based on their unique corps of salespeople who knew what the technology could do for their customers. In 1997–1998,

NCR was under pressure to find ways of reducing costs. Oblivious to this source of their monopoly, management started to lay off these salespeople as part of the cost-cutting drive. Not surprisingly, competitors snapped them up, in the process destroying NCR's situational monopoly.

We'll talk more later about ways of analyzing the monopolies you own or seek to own. For now, let's take a look at the kinds of barriers that help to create and protect monopolies.

6

BARRIERS THAT
PROTECT MONOPOLIES

The strongest forms of monopoly are those in which insurmountable barriers fence off the ownable space. Such barriers make it difficult—expensive, time-consuming, or even illegal—for competitors to enter the ownable space and destroy the monopoly.

There are three basic types of insurmountable barriers: those based on regulations that create *regulated havens;* those based on insurmountable technological barriers that create *technological havens;* and those based on customer needs and market conditions that create *customer islands.* To be most effective, a monopoly asset must lead to the creation of one of these three barriers.

REGULATION AND THE ROACH MOTEL RULE

Let's start with regulatory barriers, which can be explicit, implicit, or indirect, creating monopoly spaces by default.

Patents, trademarks, copyrights, exclusive licenses, and

outright regulation create explicit, often insurmountable barriers to entering ownable spaces. Patents make it illegal for a competitor to copy your designs or technologies, or to import products based on illegal or unauthorized copies. Patents are responsible for some of the earliest and largest monopolies. Examples include the Bell Telephone System, Xerox and Polaroid, and prescription drugs.

Trademarks and copyrights protect brand names and intellectual property, such as books, songs, and movies. Exclusive licenses protect valuable market territories, like the exclusive right to market Coca-Cola or other packaged or branded goods in a particular city or country. And explicit regulations that fence off certain industries or markets for government-owned or -regulated companies create the ultimate in insurmountable regulatory barriers.

Then there are less obvious and well-known forms of regulation—rules created and enforced by private enterprises—that can play a role in helping to establish barriers to protect monopolies. One example is a private regulation—New York Stock Exchange (NYSE) Rule 500—that bears the rather repulsive nickname of "the Roach Motel rule." I learned about it from my friend Al Berkeley, former president and chief executive officer of the all-electronic NASDAQ Stock Market. This rule has been a powerful barrier protecting the NYSE in its ongoing competition with the NASDAQ.

"The NYSE doesn't believe in competition, doesn't want competition, and will go to great lengths to prevent competi-

tion," Al told me. "The Roach Motel rule is one of the ways the NYSE makes sure that its monopoly remains intact. Essentially, the rule says that, if a firm listed on the NYSE wants to switch to the NASDAQ—or any other exchange, for that matter—it must issue a press release, send a notice to its top twenty-five stockholders, and then get approval from both the entire board and the board's audit committee." (This version of Rule 500 was put into place in 1999. The earlier version, which dated back to the 1930s, was even more onerous.)

He concluded by saying, "Now, Milind, you and I know that it's virtually impossible to meet these conditions. What the rule really means is that once a firm lists on the NYSE, it's locked in, just like the old ads for the Roach Motel bug-trap used to say: 'Roaches check in, but they don't check out.' "

TECHNOLOGICAL HAVENS

Insurmountable technological barriers are a second source of monopoly barriers. If a technology is too difficult to copy or reverse engineer, or the financial or other risks of using unauthorized copies are too high, then the ownable space is fenced off into a technological haven.

For forty years, from the mid- to late-1880s until after World War I, German chemical companies dominated the production of dyestuffs and paints. They did this by creating technological barriers reinforced by the systematic use of patents. As the scholar Ashish Arora has explained,* the German chemical players—Bayer, BASF, Hoechst, IG Farben, and others—patented a wide range of ideas covering broad areas of potential or actual interest to prevent competitive entrants from coming in. They also maintained trade secrecy to ensure that potential entrants would have to spend large sums in trial and error to replicate the results. At the same time, employees were prevented from working with competitors or would-be entrants, thereby locking up critical knowledge about processes such as the right combination of temperature and pressure, the sequence in which certain operations should be carried out, and the use of catalysts.

Net result? It took a major war to end the German monopoly. Only after Germany's defeat in World War I led to the confiscation of patents under a reparations program was DuPont able to enter the dyestuffs business. Even so, DuPont had to collaborate with a British firm that had access to a confiscated Hoechst plant, and had to hire a consultant familiar with these dyestuffs—all on top of the $11 million (a major sum in those days) that DuPont had already invested to strengthen its capabilities in dyestuffs.

Similar technological havens are not uncommon. For example, three German makers—Leitz (makers of Leica cameras), Carl Zeiss, and Schneider Kreuznach—together with Schott AG, a specialty optical glass maker, have created a

---

* Ashish Arora, "Patents, Licensing, and Market Structure in the Chemical Industry," *Research Policy*, Elsevier, vol. 26(4), pp. 391–403.

technological haven in high-performance optics. A key reason is that much of the technology in this area relates to processes that are kept trade secrets, carefully handed down from one generation of workers to the next. As one executive told me, the German workers "have something special in their fingertips." As a result, German firms dominate the high-performance niches, despite lagging in such techniques as computer-aided lens design.

Universal Oil Products (UOP) is a ninety-year-old company based in Chicago that has built a sizable technological haven by controlling process technologies used in oil refining and petrochemicals. One key to UOP's success is its patent portfolio. But equally important, UOP has nonpatented *process* expertise that would be extremely expensive to replicate. When you're investing $1 billion in a new petrochemicals complex, you really don't want to bet on an untested, unproven technology, even if you might save a few bucks. Instead, you use UOP's processes and technologies—and, of course, pay UOP for the privilege.

CUSTOMER ISLANDS

Finally, many monopolies owe their existence to barriers that create what we call *customer islands.*

About fifteen years ago, I got a call from a manager I'll call Jim Sharp. Jim was general manager of a Monsanto division that made heat transfer fluids, gooey molasses-like chemicals that transfer heat from one part of a plant to another. They're used in industries ranging from asphalt manufacturing and plastics molding to food processing. "Milind," Jim said, "we need more data on the competitive situation in our industry. We know we're number one and Dow's number two. We also *believe* that our respective market shares are 40 percent and 20 percent. But we'd like to have somebody confirm that independently. Carry out a comprehensive survey, and let me know what you find out."

My colleagues and I dutifully called nearly ten thousand users of heat transfer fluids by telephone (gross overkill, but that's another story). Three months later, I walked into a room at Monsanto where Jim and his subordinates were waiting to hear our final report.

"Gentlemen," I said, "I've got good news and bad news. The good news is that your market share estimates were accurate: The leading company does indeed control 40 percent of the market, while the number two company controls 20 percent."

Jim was beaming, as if to say "I told you so." But of course, he had to ask, "What's the bad news?"

"The bad news is that Dow is number one. Monsanto is number two!"

After Jim and his colleagues overcame their consternation over the theft of the market right from under their noses, they asked how it had happened. Fortunately, we'd uncovered the answer in the course of our research. Years earlier, Monsanto had been the leading supplier of heat transfer fluids. But for the past decade, Dow Chemical had undermined this dominance, not through advertising or by marketing their products in direct competition to Monsanto's, but by systematically courting students at all the leading colleges where chemical engineering was taught. Dow had given away free chemicals and supplies together with a very comprehensive design handbook on heat transfer. Naturally, all of the case studies and illustrative examples in the handbook were based on the use of Dowtherm, Dow's brand of heat-transfer fluids.

As a result, Dow had created a customer island—a group of highly loyal customers isolated in the overall market because of training, habit, usage patterns, geography, or brand loyalty. Dow's customer island consisted of newly graduated design engineers. As these new graduates entered the business, they increasingly dominated the field. Now, whenever an engineer designed a new plant and got around to specifying which heat transfer fluids should be used, he or she would be likely to say, "Let's see what grade of Dowtherm will do the job." Monsanto's products were rarely even considered; Dow had the key decision makers—the design engineers—all locked up!

Many powerful monopolies are based on control of customer islands—groups of near-fanatical loyalists who stick with one supplier even when they are surrounded by users of other products or services. Apple has customer islands in specific areas of computing, including art design, music, film, advertising, and other "creative" industries where Windows computers are widely scorned. Similarly, there are thousands of financial analysts who still swear by their HP-12C calculators, even though similar functions can easily be handled by personal computers and other competing devices.

In retailing, Talbot's and Nordstrom's still have customer islands, groups of extremely loyal customers that are very hard for other retailers to convert. High-mileage frequent flyers, like American Airlines' Executive Platinum members, also form customer islands; they'll fly on other airlines only when it's unavoidable. And drywall plasterers are extremely loyal to USG's Sheetrock drywall compound.

Some customer islands are sharply defined. For a long time, Midwest Express had a virtual lock on all airline travelers out of Milwaukee. In part, this was because Midwest Express offered the only nonstop service from Milwaukee to the most popular destinations. Another factor was the aura surrounding Midwest Express's service. For years it was rated the number one airline by *Travel & Leisure* magazine because of its two-and-two seating, leather seats, excellent in-flight meals, and fine cabin service. As a result, Milwaukee was a Midwest Express island.

Unique product designs can also create customer islands. BMW and Porsche own customer islands based on their appealing car designs; both are lucrative, though BMW's island is considerably larger than Porsche's. Chanel, Louis Vuitton, Coach, Burberry, Gucci, and other fashion brands have created customer islands based on their unique designs and/or perceived stylishness. Harley-Davidson has created a major cult based on its designs and even the unique "Harley sound," which the company has actually patented.

Customer islands may become especially isolated when designed-in *switching costs* discourage customers from leaving the island. For many years, the camera makers Leica and Hasselblad have enjoyed customer islands reinforced by large switching costs. Typically, Leica and Hasselblad users buy their first camera because of its design and ease of use. Over time, they buy lenses and accessories, all designed specifically for use with Leica or Hasselblad cameras. The more they invest in their cameras, the more expensive it becomes for them to switch loyalties and start all over with a Nikon or other brand.

When part of the value of a product grows out of interactions among sellers and buyers, the existence of a customer island may lead to what economists call the *network effect*. A network effect can create virtually insurmountable barriers surrounding an ownable space. Consider eBay, the leading online venue for selling or auctioning products. The popularity of eBay creates a snowballing network effect: Since eBay attracts more buyers of particular categories of goods (collectible baseball cards, for example), dealers or individuals hoping to sell to such buyers are practically forced to hawk their wares on eBay. Consequently, since nearly all sellers of baseball cards choose to advertise on eBay, anyone interested in buying from them has little choice but to visit eBay . . . and the cycle continues. In time, the result is a near-monopoly on Internet sales of collectibles for eBay.

Network effects have played a role in the creation of many monopolies. VHS videotape won its marketplace dominance over Sony's technically superior Betamax largely because of the network effect that grew from its small initial lead: During the first few years after the invention of the videotape player, more programs were available for VHS than for Beta, since the market was somewhat larger. This fact in turn attracted more buyers to VHS machines, which encouraged programmers to producer more VHS tapes, and so on.

In a similar way, the Windows operating system for personal computers owes some of its appeal to its ubiquity, which ensures that files created with Windows programs are widely compatible. A monopoly enhanced by the network effect can become almost impregnable. It's an extreme example of the power of a well-designed barrier to create the kind of long-lasting, highly profitable monopoly every business manager should seek.

7

THE NEW COMPETITION AND THE RISE OF THE SITUATIONAL MONOPOLY

ASSETS: MONOPOLY PAST

As we've seen, the company that owns a situational monopoly has no unique brands, products, or other attributes; what it does have is a *situation* that has created a monopoly. Starbucks owns a situational monopoly, having capitalized on a situation in which no other company was meeting the need for a consistent, good-tasting cup of coffee. The packaged coffee players were too focused on selling coffee in cans; local coffee shops didn't have the money or the vision to expand aggressively nationwide. Starbucks stepped into the opening and exploited the potential monopoly for all it was worth.

My research suggests that, in the future, such situational monopolies will become increasingly important, even to the point of displacing the classic asset-based monopolies. In other words, finding such *situations* will become as important as inventing new technologies, creating new products, building strong brands, or lowering total costs, if not more so. This is a sea change in business that few managers have recognized so far.

For generations, business leaders have focused their energies on creating unique assets that they hoped would provide them with an SCA—a sustainable competitive advantage. They have tried to capture control of scarce natural resources or choice business locations. They have worked to build strong mass-market brands. They have developed unique products or proprietary technologies. They have erected large plants to generate economies of scale. And they have focused obsessively on improving the efficiency of their operations in hopes of becoming low-cost providers.

At times, assets like these have helped to create monopolies and the enormous profits that go with them. Sears became *the* iconic brand in American mass-market retailing during the 1950s and 1960s largely because of its vast real-estate holdings, which included the most desirable retail locations in the newly burgeoning American suburbs. Compaq became a Fortune 500 giant thanks to an array of innovative products. Hertz and Avis developed huge scale and strong brands. Major airlines United, American, and Delta created huge hub-and-spoke networks and strong brands.

Today, however, as competition intensifies in industry after industry, such monopoly assets are losing their effectiveness at generating high profits. At the same time, facing the same intense competition in the same industries, companies with situational monopolies are thriving.

Even as Sears is struggling in retailing, Wal-Mart keeps on growing and recently whizzed past $250 billion in annual revenues. In the world of PCs and, now, consumer electronics, Dell is gobbling up rivals and market share; Compaq, yesterday's iconic brand, is history. Enterprise Rent-A-Car has the largest fleet in North America and is arguably the most profitable company in its industry. And Southwest and JetBlue have created large airlines that are far more profitable than the so-called majors.

KODAK MEETS THE NEW COMPETITION

The reason for this changing of the guard is the emergence of the New Competition—the most wrenching series of economic changes since the original Industrial Revolution a hundred and fifty years ago. *Everything* is changing rapidly in unexpected, often totally unanticipated ways.

Globalization is opening up vast new markets and creating an army of powerful new competitors. Globalization is also transmitting skills, processes, and technologies all over the world, making it very easy for companies in every corner of the globe to copy product features, designs, even entire technologies—legally and illegally. Powerful buyers are driving down prices and reshaping the value relationships in many industries, abetted by eager low-cost suppliers from

China, India, Brazil, and other developing nations. Finally, consumer needs are changing in unprecedented ways, driven by the aging population of the West and the emergence of vast numbers of young consumers in the East.

In this unstable environment, traditional asset monopolies are at a huge disadvantage. It takes time to build a brand, develop a new product, or bring a technology to market. By the time the brand, product, or technology is ready, the industry situation, competitive landscape, or customer requirements is likely to have changed. The traditional company focused solely on assets is like a big, lumbering American football lineman who suddenly finds himself in the middle of a soccer match. He doesn't know the rules, he doesn't know how to recognize scoring opportunities, and his huge size and brute strength are suddenly liabilities rather than assets. No wonder the New Competition is devastating the old monopolies.

Consider Kodak. For nearly a century, Kodak *was* the American film industry. It controlled the technology and enjoyed incredible advantages of scale and brand. To most Americans (and to many other consumers around the world), there was no such thing as photo film that didn't come in a bright yellow cardboard box.

In the last fifteen years, Kodak's asset-based monopoly has unraveled. First, Fuji entered the United States market and created real price competition. Fuji was quite different from Agfa-Gevaert, Ilford, GAF, or Polaroid, Kodak's traditional competitors. Like Kodak, Fuji was vertically integrated, technologically sophisticated, and enjoyed the benefits of a huge, captive home market. Fuji also had something Kodak lacked—connections with leading-edge camera makers. These assets made Fuji by far the most formidable opponent Kodak had ever faced.

Then Kodak's traditional mom-and-pop corner drug-stores and photography dealers began to lose their markets to chain stores, including Walgreens, Kroger, Publix and, later on, Wal-Mart, causing a further price and profit squeeze on Kodak. The crowning blow was the advent of digital photography in the late 1990s, which devastated Kodak's traditional business model based on selling, processing, and printing film. Kodak brings no assets to the digital table. It owns no unique software, no skills related to the manufacture of digital cameras, and no proprietary products like sensors or electronics of value to other digital photography players. No wonder Kodak is struggling to figure out how it will make money in the New Competition.

The global music industry is another symbol of how the New Competition will devastate the old monopolies. In 1999, the music industry was riding a wave. Revenues and profits had been growing nicely since 1980, when the audio CD was introduced, and sales had reached a record high of $41 billion. Then in June 1999, a teenaged Northeastern University student named Shawn Fanning launched an online music-sharing service called Napster.

The music business hasn't been the same since. Consumers realized that a CD priced at $16.95 costs less than a buck to make (not counting royalties to the artists and performers). They also noticed that file sharing let them download just the two or three songs they really liked from an album without having to buy another dozen tunes stuck in as fillers. With the Internet making it very easy to swap songs, music buyers suddenly had the means, the motive, and the opportunity to bypass the record industry's music monopoly. As a result, worldwide music sales have declined every year for the last four years; in 2003, they were $31 billon, down more than 20 percent from their 1999 peak. Profit margins have collapsed, major record labels have consolidated, and several music retailers have filed for bankruptcy.

SITUATIONS: MONOPOLY FUTURE

If Kodak and the music industry are monopoly past, the personal computer industry is nightmare present.

Thanks to intense competition and rapid diffusion of technologies, it's very hard to make any real money in PCs today. Every PC maker buys the same components from the same suppliers, uses the same contract manufacturers, and sells them through the same channels to the same groups of customers. Consequently, new designs, new features, new marketing campaigns, and new (generally lower) prices all ripple quickly through the industry, making it virtually impossible to create a monopoly space.

Consequently, the only players making any significant profits in or around the PC business are Microsoft and Intel, which have asset monopolies based on their technologies; Apple, which has a large customer island populated by fanatically loyal Apple-heads; and Dell, which has . . . a situational monopoly.

The truth is that the decade to come is likely to be the golden age of the situational monopoly.

As we've seen, the intense pressures of the New Competition are making it almost impossible to sustain an asset monopoly in most industries. Competing firms from around the world are watching your every move and stand ready to copy your products, your designs, and your technologies at a moment's notice. Yet ironically, *because* the managers in every company are watching the competition so closely, they may be oblivious to situational opportunities that are staring them in the face.

Take car rental. Early on, Hertz, Avis, and National monopolized the real estate at every airport. They had the counters, the locations, and the network. Building on this powerful set of assets, they created additional incentives to keep customers loyal—frequent renter programs, expedited rentals, and discounts for vacationers. As competition heated up, other rental companies entering the market copied the majors. They demanded *their* counter space at the airports and offered customer loyalty programs of their own. As the differences among car rental companies blurred, competition led to commoditization.

Ironically, they were all so intent on watching one another (and imitating the tangible assets each company created) that they missed the situational monopoly Enterprise Rent-A-Car tapped into—the replacement car market that Enterprise seized.

As the competition increases in other industries, we will see the same pattern emerge. Traditional, asset-based monopolies will become less and less effective at generating high profits, and the new success stories will be companies like Enterprise Rent-A-Car and JetBlue, which find and exploit the open spaces that everyone else is overlooking. Increasingly, tomorrow's monopolies will be situational.

DELL DEFEATS THE I.T. NAZI

When I speak about Dell to classes of MBA students, they're all convinced that they understand the secrets behind Dell's success. The moment I call for volunteers, the hands shoot up:

"They have the lowest costs of any PC manufacturer. They've got their supply chain working tighter than a drum."

"They build to order. They carry virtually no inventory. They turn their working capital thirty times a year and have very little investment in manufacturing plants."

"They've eliminated the costs of the dealer channel by going direct. That's why they can price so competitively and still make money."

"They have low prices with great customer service."

All true. But these factors don't explain how Dell grew from a $10 million business to a $1 billion business. They don't tell us how Michael Dell became *Michael Dell.* After all, when Dell Computer got started, it didn't have the size or scope to create a price advantage over IBM or Compaq. And it had no traditional sustainable competitive advantage—no unique product, technology, or brand. So what was the key to Dell's success?

When I pressed one of my MBA classes for an answer, it came from the lone engineer in the room—a rumpled older guy I'll call Charlie.

"Dell helped me beat the IT Nazi," Charlie said.

"Sounds like a *Seinfeld* episode," I quipped.

"In a way," Charlie agreed. "When I was starting out in product engineering, if I wanted a computer fitted out the way I wanted it, I had two choices. I could go to the MIS director and ask her to get me a Compaq with a math co-processor, extra memory, a bigger hard drive, and all the other things I needed. Then we'd have an argument about why I couldn't make do with what everyone else was using. We'd go round and round until she finally gave in. Six weeks later, I'd get my machine. If I was lucky."

"And that's why you called her the IT Nazi."

"You got it."

"What was your other choice?"

"I could avoid the arguments by spending three weeks looking through a bunch of catalogs and assembling my own system."

Charlie took a sip of water. "Then Dell came along. Now all I had to do was pick up the phone, tell them what I wanted, give them my corporate charge number, and within three days I had it."

Another student chimed in. "What about the IT Nazi? Didn't she object to you bypassing her?"

"Nah," said Charlie with a shrug. "She never knew a

thing. My boss had his own budget and he and I just set up the account with Dell."

"What about Compaq?" I asked. "Didn't they offer you the same service as Dell?"

"No, and they still don't. They say they do, but their system is more complicated, more hassle, and more expensive. That's how Dell got to be so big. Dell got a monopoly on our business."

If any of Dell's larger, more powerful, better-known competitors had responded to the needs of engineers like Charlie, there would have been no monopoly, no above-average profits, no *Michael Dell!* Instead, they allowed a situation to exist in which upstart Dell, with no unique assets, was able to seize and hold a profitable monopoly space. That space, in turn, became the basis for what is now the largest and most profitable company in the PC industry.

THE EGG BEATERS MONOPOLY

Egg Beaters was another classic situational monopoly. The company that created it, Standard Brands, owned no unique technology or other tangible monopoly asset. Yet for years, Egg Beaters was the *only* cholesterol-free egg substitute in the supermarket dairy case.

Peter Rogers, CEO of Standard Brands when Egg Beaters was launched in the mid-1970s, explains how it happened. "Egg Beaters is essentially just egg whites with some food coloring to give the end product, whether it's scrambled eggs or an omelet, that characteristic yellow flavor. There was no particular technology or patent protecting us. Anybody could have copied the product."

In the world of packaged goods, heavy consumer advertising is the traditional approach to building awareness of a new brand. Standard Brands chose not to follow this route. Instead, it went to the physicians and educated them about the benefits of Egg Beaters for their patients with high cholesterol. In so doing, Standard Brands was repeating the strategy it had used earlier to reposition Fleischmann's margarine as a cholesterol-free substitute for butter.

Standard Brands' timing was excellent. Heart disease had been receiving enormous publicity as a major cause of death among Americans and consequently, everyone—especially men in their 40s—was concerned about cholesterol. And in the mid-1970s, almost everyone still ate eggs for breakfast. "So here was this segment of consumers," Peter recalls, "mostly male, who were suddenly being told to lay off eggs because they have too much cholesterol. These consumers were natural targets for a low-cholesterol egg."

It all sounds so obvious. So why didn't the competition follow Egg Beaters? The reason was myopia, based on preexisting assumptions about the product development path. Peter explains, "Basically, everyone else in the food industry was focused on soy-based substitutes for eggs. They just couldn't or wouldn't abandon their research investments in soy. But soy eggs didn't work. They just didn't taste like eggs. That left us [Standard Brands] all alone on the dairy shelf."

As the Egg Beaters story illustrates, a situational monopoly exists when you have something consumers are willing to pay for, and no one else is willing or able to match your offer. This combination of an unmet need and competitor inertia creates an uncanny situation in which it's possible to earn *monopoly profits from a commodity product!*

In a situational monopoly, conventional assets such as product differentiation, a strong brand, a unique technology, or low cost are largely irrelevant. The reasoning is simple: If you have something people want, *and no one else is meeting that need,* people will buy from you. The product or service doesn't have to be cheap, unique, or widely advertised. As movie director Woody Allen once said, "Eighty percent of success is showing up." When you have a situational monopoly, all you have to do is show up.

8

MONOPOLIES DRIVE
MARKET VALUE

GOOGLE'S STOCK OPERA

Time for a small side trip.

Up to this point, we've been considering the importance of monopoly strictly from the point of view of the business manager—the CEO, chief marketing officer, brand manager, or other executive with an interest in competitive strategy.

But because monopoly is so central to business success, it's also a valuable concept for anyone interested in probing the ultimate sources of corporate valuation. This includes individual investors, portfolio managers, managers of endowment funds, chief financial officers, and anyone else who needs to know what makes the stock market tick. (Of course, understanding the forces that drive corporate valuation is also increasingly important to business managers in an era when more and more companies are measuring their success by the market value of their stock—and compensating managers accordingly.)

As a way of approaching the connection between monopoly power and stock valuation, let's consider one of the most famous new stocks to hit the market in recent years— Google, the dominant player in the burgeoning Internet search engine business.

Google's initial public stock offering (IPO) was one of the biggest, most raucous multimedia circuses of 2004— a kind of opéra bouffe, complete with angry baritones storming about the stage (investment bankers and mutual fund managers), strong-willed prima donnas stamping their feet (Google's managers and owners), and a confused, adoring, carping cast of thousands milling about aimlessly (investors like you and me). And like any good opéra bouffe, it had a happy ending, with Google going public at $85 a share and finishing its first day of trading at $100.34 for a nice, respectable gain of 18 percent.

The theme of the opera, of course, was good, old-fashioned greed. The investment banks were miffed at being bypassed in Google's unusual direct-to-investors, auction-style IPO—and no wonder, since they were deprived of hundreds of millions of dollars in fees. The institutional investors were angry that they weren't allowed to play their usual lucrative game of grabbing most of the shares of a popular IPO at bargain basement prices and turning right around and selling them for big first-day profits. And Google's management was angry with investment bankers and institutional investors for demanding a low price, causing Google to leave money on the table. As usual, greed brought out the worst in everyone.

But behind all the hoopla and histrionics about the role

of investment bankers, the irrationality of individual investors, and the long-term dangers of auctions, was the age-old, fundamental investment question, "What is Google *really* worth?" Is Google worth $115 a share (as its managers suggested early on) or is the actual issue price of $85 closer to reality? And what will happen to Google's stock price when Microsoft launches its own search engine, or when Yahoo!'s new search service takes off?

MONOPOLY AND MARKET VALUE

To answer these questions, we need to look at the power of Google's monopoly. Our hypothesis is this: *Monopoly drives a company's stock market value.* Why might this be so? It's simple: the high returns that a company enjoys from a monopoly carry with them few or no financial risks. Therefore, the more a business looks like a perfect, unregulated monopoly, the more investors should be willing to pay for it. Furthermore, a company's market value should also be correlated with the size and duration of its monopoly space. The larger its monopoly customer base and the longer the monopoly is likely to last, the more investors should be willing to pay.

To test this hypothesis, let's begin with a look at Microsoft, which is as close to an unregulated monopoly as you can get. As of this writing (December 2004), Microsoft is trading on the NASDAQ exchange at a price of over $27 per share. Based on the company's annualized sales and the total number of shares outstanding, it's possible to calculate that

Microsoft is currently pulling in revenues of a little over $3.30 per share. When you divide the share price ($27) by the revenues per share ($3.30), you discover that Microsoft is selling for over eight times revenues. In other words, Wall Street likes Microsoft's stock so much that it pays more than eight dollars for every dollar in revenue the company generates.

This sounds impressive. How does it compare with another great company, Coca-Cola? As we've seen, Coke has enjoyed a near monopoly over the cola space for more than a century, based on the combination of its brand image and its special product (the "secret formula" and all that). As I write, Coca-Cola shares are trading at just over $40. When we perform the calculations, we find that Coke is selling for just under four and a half times revenues. Not as high as Microsoft, but still pretty high.

Before going any further, let me point out some facts for those who may not be particularly well versed in stock market fundamentals. The ratio I've been focusing on—share price versus company revenues per share—is a basic and widely used stock value indicator. It's generally referred to as the *price-to-sales ratio* or P/S.

It's not necessary for an individual investor to perform his or her own calculations to determine a stock's P/S ratio because the number is widely available through sources such as the Morningstar and Value Line information services. Throughout this chapter, the P/S ratios I'll cite will be those provided by Morningstar as of December 5, 2004. Naturally, P/S ratios, like other stock indicators, change from day to day. But for most large companies, their short-term fluctuations will be modest.

So Microsoft boasts a P/S ratio over 8.0, while Coke's is just under 4.5. What about Starbucks, the Coke of the twenty-somethings? Its P/S ratio is very comparable to Coke's, currently at 4.74. On the other hand, United Parcel Service, which owns the ground parcel business but faces stiff competition in overnight package deliveries and international shipping, sells for just 2.76 times revenues.

The numbers we are uncovering are beginning to suggest a relationship: The more your business looks like a pure monopoly—the closer it gets to Microsoft—the more Wall Street is willing to pay for a dollar of revenue.

A few more examples. Estée Lauder owns the cosmetics counter in finer department stores (Nordstrom, Bloomingdale's, and the like). Consequently, its market value is just a little shy of two times revenues (a P/S ratio of 1.80). Competitor Revlon, on the other hand, is valued much lower, at around 61¢ for every dollar of revenue, despite owning the cosmetics counter at Walgreens and Wal-Mart. Essentially, investors are saying to Ron Perelman, Revlon's controlling shareholder, "Ron, you may own the cosmetics counter at Wal-Mart, but Wal-Mart will squeeze all the profits out of you. So we don't think your monopoly is worth much."

Of course, there's no real mystery in the relationship between monopoly and market value. Investors reward profits; the more profitable a company or an investment, the more people are willing to pay for a piece of it. And as we've seen in the previous chapters of this book, any business that earns above-average profits *must* own some monopoly, somewhere. The larger the ownable space (the more customers and revenue it contains) and the longer the company will own it exclusively, the greater the value of the business. No ownable space and no monopoly period means no above-average profits, and, consequently, no investor interest. That's why monopoly drives market value.

What's more, investors are looking for *future* profits; in this context, history doesn't matter (except as a *possible* indicator of future profit potential). What investors want to know is, "How big will the profit pie be *tomorrow?*" A tiny, local monopoly that isn't growing very fast is less valuable and attracts fewer investors than a large regional or national monopoly that's doubling in size every two or three years.

We see these relationships played out in the real world continually. During 2004, Apple Computer's stock price went from just under $20 per share to over $60, more than tripling its market value. The reason? The enormous popularity of the iPod music player, Apple's most valuable current monopoly. Between the second and third quarters of the year, iPod sales *quintupled,* reaching over two million units in the quarter ending September 25, 2004.

Of course, Apple investors loved this picture. The only real question in their minds was "How long will this last? How long will Apple own this space?" Most analysts assumed that Apple's future monopoly period would be a year or less, since other equipment makers had already begun to promote their own versions of the iPod, and the 800-pound gorilla of infotech, Microsoft, was known to be mounting an assault on Apple's complementary iTunes online music distribution site. Everyone assumed that once Microsoft entered the music business in full force, Apple's monopoly would soon vanish. If investors ever become convinced that Apple's jukebox monopoly will last, the stock price will go even higher.

By the way, Apple's P/S ratio is currently a little over three—3.23, to be exact. So the stock is trading at a nice premium to company revenues, though not at the level of Microsoft, Coca-Cola, or Starbucks.

MQ: THE MONOPOLY QUOTIENT

One way we can measure the market value of a monopoly is through a rating I refer to as the *Monopoly Quotient* (MQ). Strictly speaking, this isn't a quotient, as it is not the ratio of two numbers. I choose to call it MQ because of the parallelism with such familiar terms as "IQ," which measures intelligence, and "EQ," which measures so-called emotional intelligence.

We define MQ as the monopoly period in years (let's call it M), multiplied by the annual sales growth rate (let's call it R). In other words:

$$MQ = \text{Monopoly period (M)} \times \text{Annual sales growth rate (R)}$$
$$MQ = M \times R$$

MQ is a pure percentage; it tells us how much the company's "monopoly revenues" will grow during its monopoly period. It's a quick and dirty way of estimating the size of the future monopoly pie.

To go back to the Apple iPod example, if iPod sales are growing at 50 percent per year, and we think that Apple's iPod monopoly will last three years from today, we'd calculate Apple's MQ this way:

$$MQ = M \times R$$
$$MQ = 3 \times 0.5 = 1.5$$

Apple's monopoly quotient of 1.5 is the equivalent of 150 percent, meaning that Apple's monopoly revenues—and by extension, Apple's monopoly profits—will be multiplied one and a half times their present levels.

Obviously, MQ ignores various complications such as compounding of growth (50 percent a year compounded over three years is 237 percent, not 150 percent), profits vs. revenues, the possibility that revenue growth rates might change, uncertainty about the actual monopoly period, and other factors. But it is a useful, rough-and-ready approximation.

Before we can use the MQ to measure the market value of a monopoly, we have to calibrate it. This means correlating MQ with a company's market value as a percentage of its sales—its P/S ratio. (Unavoidably, the following discussion will be a little technical and dry.)

To calibrate the MQ, we'll use data from the prescription drug industry. Why? Because in prescription drugs, the data needed to calculate MQ is unusually accessible.

First of all, in the pharmaceutical industry, the monopoly period (M) is clear and well-defined, since it is based on the average future lifespan of the firm's major outstanding patents. Conveniently, this time frame is also available to investors because the relevant data are contained in regulatory filings with the FDA. The revenue growth rate (R) is also relatively easy to calculate. Thanks to public health statistics, we have a reasonably good idea of the total number of patients suffering from a particular disease or condition, and how fast this number is growing. From this data, we can estimate how much of a particular drug they will purchase. We can use this data to calculate MQ and compare it against the company's market value as measured by its current price-to-sales (P/S) ratio.

For this exercise, we'll consider five pharmaceutical firms that represent a reasonably representative swath of a highly varied industry.

Let's start with Amgen, an early biotech pioneer with several patented drugs that have rapidly growing sales. Amgen's patent portfolio has an average span of ten-plus years left before it expires, so we can peg Amgen's monopoly period at approximately 10. Amgen's revenues have been growing at around 25 percent per year, so its sales growth rate (R) is 25 percent or 0.25. This means that Amgen's monopoly quotient (MQ) is 2.5 (10×0.25), or 250 percent. Finally, we discover (through a moment's research on Morningstar.com) that Amgen's current P/S ratio is 8.39, which means that investors are willing to pay over eight times annual revenues for Amgen's stock—a handsome premium.

Next, let's look at Pfizer, which has several blockbuster drugs (as they're known in pharmaceutical industry parlance).

Pfizer's patent portfolio also has more than ten years to go before it expires, so its monopoly period (M) equals 10. Pfizer's sales have been growing at around 15 percent per year, meaning R is 15 percent or 0.15. Pfizer's MQ then is 1.5 (10 × 0.15). The company's P/S ratio is 3.98.

By contrast, Bristol-Myers and Merck have patent portfolios that will expire within two to three years, and their sales are growing much more slowly; consequently their MQ's are low. IVAX is a generic drug maker; as such, its monopoly period is very short and its sales are growing slowly too, so its MQ is quite low. All of the information for the five companies is shown in the table below.

Company	M	R	MQ	P/S
MQ AND P/S RATIOS FOR MAJOR PRESCRIPTION DRUG MANUFACTURERS				
Amgen	10	0.25	2.50	8.39
Pfizer	10	0.15	1.50	3.98
Merck	3	0.07	0.21	2.76
Bristol-Myers	3	0.05	0.15	2.14
IVAX	2	0.03	0.06	2.44

As you can see, there is a rough correlation between the last two columns in our table. It confirms what we suspected—that Wall Street tends to price stocks in accordance with the perceived future earning power of their monopolies. In the case of these pharmaceutical firms, where MQ can be calculated with a fair degree of accuracy, Amgen has both the highest MQ and the highest P/S ratio. Pfizer is second on both counts, Merck third, while Bristol-Myers and IVAX bring up the rear.

Of course, this analysis of the pharmaceutical industry is admittedly rudimentary. One could extend it by including more companies and perhaps by adding one or two other popular share price indicators, such as the price-to-earnings ratio (P/E). But this deeper level of detail wouldn't alter the fundamental relationship between stock price premium and monopoly strength.

SO WHAT'S GOOGLE *REALLY* WORTH?

Now let's see how Google compares.

Over the last twelve months, Google's revenues have rocketed up at an annual rate of 233 percent. But common sense tells us that it's too much to expect that Google's revenues will double or triple every year, so let's trim the growth rate to a more moderate 50 percent per year. (This is still an extraordinary growth rate. If it comes true, Google's revenues will grow from $1.47 billion in 2003 to over $11 billion in 2008.)

Google's monopoly period is harder to estimate, with Microsoft and Yahoo! already developing their own competitive search technologies. So let's be fairly generous and say that Google will have the search market to itself for another three years.

With an R of 0.5 and an M of 3, Google's MQ is 1.5. As of this writing, Google stock is trading at over $177 per share, giving it a P/S ratio of over 21 (see table below).

MQ AND P/S RATIO FOR GOOGLE				
Company	M	R	MQ	P/S
Google	3	0.50	1.50	21.04

How does this compare to our drug company table? Google has the same MQ as Pfizer, 1.50. That suggests that if Google were a drug stock, it should probably have a P/S ratio in line with Pfizer's, or around four times revenues. At that multiple, Google's stock would be selling closer to $34 per share, rather than its current price of $177.

What if we make our projections for Google's monopoly more generous? Even if Google's sales double every year—in other words, if R = 1.0 rather than 0.5—Google's MQ would be only 3.0. Consequently, its price-to-sales ratio, judging by the pharmaceutical industry comparison, would be only somewhat higher than Amgen's—perhaps ten times revenues. That still means that Google's stock should be more like $84 a share rather than $177.

Another way of looking at this question is to *start* with Google's price-to-sales ratio and work backwards. By extrapolating from Amgen and Pfizer, we see that Google's P/S ratio of 21 suggests a monopoly quotient around 6.0. This means that to justify its current price premium, Google should double its revenues every year *and* face no significant competition from Microsoft, Yahoo!, or anybody else for the next six years. Otherwise, Google stock is overpriced.

As this exercise illustrates, because of patents and the information required by FDA regulations, prescription drugs are the closest approximation on Wall Street to the ideal benchmark—a monopoly with revenues, profits, and monopoly period that are known in advance. Consequently, the P/S ratios for prescription drugs can be treated as a ceiling, an upper bound. For a given monopoly quotient, a rational investor shouldn't be willing to pay more (that is, accept a higher P/S ratio) than for a prescription drug stock with the same MQ. In fact, if there's any uncertainty about the company's prospects, we should demand a *discount* from the prescription drug stock's P/S ratio.

Time alone will tell whether Google is overpriced or will continue to grow as rapidly as investors apparently think it will. But our Google discussion shows the value of the monopoly quotient, MQ, in thinking about a company's *real* market value (what value investors like Warren Buffett term its "intrinsic worth"). Calculating MQ forces us to ask some basic questions about the company: "What is the monopoly driving this company's growth? How long will this monopoly last and why? How is Wall Street valuing its monopoly? Is this valuation reasonable?" We can then make up our own ideas about a particular stock and decide whether, at the current price, the stock is a sell or a buy.

Before you rush off and start picking stocks using MQ, a word of caution. First, remember that our pharmaceutical benchmark is quite rudimentary. The calculations we use have the advantage of simplicity; all you need to do is estimate the likely monopoly period and find out how fast the company's sales have been growing. But our system doesn't take into account the fact that drug companies are extremely profitable, while steel companies, car makers, and packaged goods makers (for example) are much less so.

Second, stock prices are volatile. MQ offers one tentative measurement of the *long-term* market value of a company. But on any given day, rumors, euphoria, pessimism, or optimism about a particular sector or about the economy as a whole drive the prices of individual shares all over the map. You have to understand these swings and make your own trading decisions.

MQ is just a single tool for examining the long-term growth prospects of a particular company and, therefore, its future market value. But potentially it's a very useful one because it's the *first* stock market indicator that focuses on the extraordinary power of monopoly to build and sustain a business.

9

MONOPOLY KALEIDOSCOPE

TED TURNER AND THE CNN MONOPOLY

Monopoly is like a kaleidoscope. One moment you see a beautiful pattern that is generating monopoly profits for some lucky company. Then the kaleidoscope turns, and the monopoly is gone. In its place you see chaos, no pattern at all—in other words, a commodity marketplace where products, services, and supplies do battle with no dominant market leader. But when the kaleidoscope turns yet again, a new pattern emerges, often with a totally different monopoly.

Three key dynamics—*industry shifts, competitor shifts,* and *customer shifts*—are responsible. The interactions of these three forces destroy old monopolies and create new ones. When the changes are gradual, existing players have time to adapt. Often, however, industry structures, competitor behaviors, and customer needs change quickly and unexpectedly. As a result, new players emerge, often playing a whole new ballgame.

Media entrepreneur Ted Turner, founder of Turner Broadcasting System (TBS), launched CNN on June 1, 1980.

Most observers considered it a long shot—an upstart network operating on a shoestring budget with no celebrities and limited experience, testing the unproven proposition that Americans were hungry for TV news twenty-four hours a day. But by 1985, CNN was reaching more than 33 million households—nearly 40 percent of all American homes, and four out of five cable subscribers. Five years after that, CNN had become a globally respected news source on a par with the broadcast networks. CNN had arrived.

More important from a business perspective, CNN was a monopoly. For sixteen years, until Fox News was launched in 1996, CNN had no competition—it was the *only* all-news cable channel. Internationally, CNN had an even more dramatic monopoly. Especially in countries with state-run broadcast monopolies, CNN provided the *only unbiased* source of TV news.

THE THREE DYNAMICS: CUSTOMER, COMPETITOR, AND INDUSTRY SHIFTS

The story of how industry, competitor, and customer dynamics interacted to create a new monopoly opportunity, how news novice Ted Turner seized this opportunity, and why the established players didn't respond more quickly, is a vivid example of the monopoly kaleidoscope in motion.

The seeds of CNN's monopoly were sown in a series of seemingly unrelated shifts starting in the early 1970s.

The first was the development of satellite TV. The first

satellite television signal had been relayed from Europe to the Telstar satellite over North America in 1962. The first domestic North American satellite to carry television was Canada's Anik 1, launched in 1973. As the seventies progressed, satellite uplinks and downlinks became increasingly available all over the world, even behind the Iron Curtain. Soon the villager in Azerbaijan could see what was happening in Zanzibar on his television screen, and vice versa.

Most important, the availability of relatively low-cost, high-capacity satellite links meant that *national*, as opposed to local or regional, cable networks became viable. Individual systems could put up a satellite dish and download cable programs at low cost; they didn't have to be large enough to develop their own programming or rely on the traditional broadcast networks.

A second key development was improved technology for recording, transmitting, and viewing TV images. Thanks to lighter, tougher, and cheaper cameras and sound recording equipment, more news could be captured and recorded in far-flung locations with less investment and, in many cases, with higher quality of picture and sound. Transmission equipment also became lighter, less expensive, and more robust, while the same technology made home TV sets cheaper and more reliable. Consequently, when large markets like India and China opened up for TV, millions of locals could afford to buy their own sets. And buy they did, creating huge new markets for programming in sports, entertainment—and news.

In turn, these technological changes drove regulatory changes in the United States and around the world. While the pattern and the pace of change varied from country to country, the net result was the same: Long-established operators such as North America's ABC, NBC, and CBS; England's BBC; France Télévisions; the German state-owned networks ARD and ZDF; and India's Doordarshan found themselves competing for viewers with upstarts like Turner's TBS, Rupert Murdoch's SkyTV, and specialized programmers ranging from MTV and ESPN to HBO and the Home Shopping Network.

As a result of these changes, the focus of the TV industry shifted from capacity to content. When broadcast was the only way to transmit a TV signal, capacity was a scarce resource. There were only two, three, or four channels on which to broadcast, and only a few hours a day when broadcasting was considered economically viable. Those who owned this limited capacity—the broadcast networks—controlled the industry.

Cable created capacity that was almost unlimited. The typical cable system could carry a hundred or more channels. Now the problem was finding enough content to fill the capacity. Unless there was something new, different, and interesting to watch, why would anyone pay a premium for cable service? Inevitably, power started moving from those who owned the capacity to those who owned the content—companies like Disney, Fox, Time Warner, Viacom, and others. News had the potential to become one of the major content streams attracting cable and satellite viewership.

At the same time, viewers' needs and habits were changing, driven by changes in the family and in society. The tradition of the evening news broadcast anchored by a "national uncle" like Walter Cronkite or David Brinkley was rooted in the post–World War II era of the nuclear family. Dad worked, Mom stayed at home, and the kids went to school. When six o'clock rolled around, families gathered by their TV sets to catch up on the day's events. It was a cozy tradition many TV executives assumed would endure forever.

But by the late 1970s, many nuclear families were morphing into new and unfamiliar forms. Millions of moms had joined the workforce; single-parent families were on the rise; the lives of kids were increasingly filled with after-school activities that replaced family time with organized events and hours spent in the car. TV viewing began to shift from a fixed time and a fixed place to any time, any place. The six o'clock news was poised to go the way of the home-cooked meatloaf dinner, to be replaced by the microwaved entrée and the all-news, all-the-time cable channel.

The final ingredient needed to create the monopoly opportunity for Ted Turner was competitor inertia. The industry's incumbent powers—ABC, CBS, and NBC—failed to respond to the industry and customer shifts. There were a number of reasons for this inertia. One was simple complacency. For nearly three decades, the networks had maintained an extremely profitable oligopoly, protected from serious competition by regulation and the technological limits of broadcasting. Taking their power for granted, they failed to recognize that the new technologies of cable and satellite television were outstripping regulatory change. More ominously, they failed to notice that the cable players were well organized politically, meaning that when regulatory change *did* arrive, it would shatter the networks' oligopoly forever.

A second reason was lack of focus. News was a small, not very profitable part of the networks' overall programming portfolio. It was costly to gather and report news, especially internationally. Consequently, the networks considered their news operations loss leaders that brought prestige and fulfilled the mandate for "public service" imposed on them by the Federal Communications Commission (FCC), but earned little money. The networks had scant incentive to expand the amount of airtime devoted to news, let alone create an all-news channel.

More fundamentally, the networks failed to envision the underlying economics of an all-news operation like CNN. As one CNN executive explained, "If CBS sends someone to Timbuktu to cover a story, they can use it maybe two or three times. If we send someone to cover the same story, we reuse it twenty or thirty times—ten to twelve times on CNN, a few more times on CNN International, a few more times on Headline News, and so on. In the end, our cost per story is a fraction of CBS's."

THE CHAIN REACTION

Monopolies form and disappear as a result of a chain reaction. Normally, changes in the three dynamics of industry, competitor, and customer are required. These changes also need to occur more or less simultaneously so as to reinforce one another.

Suppose the television universe had experienced industry and competitor changes like those that created the cable and satellite networks, but no change in viewers' habits. It's likely there would have been no real demand for an all-news network and therefore no new monopoly opportunity.

If viewer demands had changed, but without the array of technology-driven changes in the industry, there would have been no widespread cable networks and, again, no monopoly opportunity for CNN.

Finally, if the industry and customer shifts had occurred but the traditional competitors—CBS, ABC, and NBC—had been quick to respond, we would have had three or more all-news cable channels (in 1980 rather than twenty years later). Once again, no chance to create a monopoly.

Thus, it's the *interaction among all three dynamics* that created the monopoly opportunity Ted Turner seized. Without that interaction, you don't get the chain reaction that creates space for a new monopoly.

Toyota, Nissan, and Honda entered the American market in the mid-sixties and offered small, fuel-efficient cars with superior quality and value to those produced by American automakers. But they made little headway until the winter of 1981–1982, when the second international oil crisis precipitated a shift in the customer dynamic. Fed up with gas shortages and the high cost of a fill-up, Americans began to value fuel efficiency more than ever before. Around the same time, a shift in the industry dynamic gave the kaleidoscope an additional push: The Japanese automakers began to offer full-size cars.

This combination of factors produced the explosion. Between 1983 and 1985, the share of the American auto market held by General Motors fell from 46 percent to 36 percent—*a drop of nearly a quarter of GM's total sales volume!* The Japanese automakers snatched up the difference.

Kodak's saga over the past two decades is a textbook example of how monopolies form, change, and disappear. For sixty-plus years, from the 1920s to the mid-1980s, Kodak monopolized the North American film and photofinishing market. As we've already noted, this monopoly started to unravel in the late 1970s. As is typical in these situations, Kodak's managers responded to individual symptoms without fully grasping the gravity of the problem. Consequently, they were unable to protect their old monopoly, nor were they able to identify and capitalize on emerging new monopoly spaces.

The first cracks in Kodak's monopoly appeared when competitor dynamics changed. Fuji's entry into the market gave film retailers their first real alternative to Kodak. Then the industry dynamic changed. Large chain stores started claiming an ever-larger share of film and photofinishing sales. These retailers used their enormous volume and the recent entry of Fuji into the market to squeeze Kodak on price, and squeeze they did.

The next ingredient in the chain reaction was a change in the customer dynamic. By the mid-1980s, the baby boom generation had largely outgrown its inherited reluctance to buy foreign goods. They had had good experiences with products from Toyota, Honda, Sony, and Panasonic. Why not try a camera film from Japan?

The advent of digital photography completed Kodak's nightmare. Digital was the final blow to the remnants of Kodak's film monopoly. It killed everything—film, disposable cameras, and, to a large extent, photofinishing.

In response, Kodak's managers made two crucial errors. First, they were slow to recognize how the various dynamics were changing. As a result, they failed to adapt to the changes, let alone anticipate them. Second, they kept investing in familiar technologies rather than the emerging digital technologies. For example, in 1988 Kodak spent nearly $4 billion to acquire Sterling Drug. (The acquisition never panned out; Kodak finally sold off the company in 1994.)

As a result, Kodak didn't have enough money to invest when digital photography took off in the late 1990s. At the time, they could have bought Adobe Systems for less than half of what they paid for Sterling Drug. Thanks to Photoshop, the dominant software for editing and printing digital pictures, Adobe owns digital photography. Today Adobe's market value is 70 percent of Kodak's . . . on a *tenth* of Kodak's revenues.

THE MORAL OF THE STORY

What's the moral of the CNN, Japanese carmaker, and Kodak stories for incumbent businesses? It's twofold. First, you can never afford to be complacent. Every business is subject to the changes generated by the monopoly kaleidoscope. Companies that manage to maintain their monopolies for a generation or more do so only by continually adapting to their shifting environments.

Second, you need to be constantly scanning the horizon for the three kinds of changes we've identified in this chapter: changes in industry dynamics (which may be driven by new technologies, legal and regulatory changes, or other structural shifts); changes in competitor behavior (such as the emergence of new rivals, the collapse of old ones, or a dramatic shift in strategy by an important industry player); and changes in customer needs (often based on demographic, economic, and cultural movements).

When one shift occurs, you need to start developing your response. When two shifts occur, it's time to counterattack. When three shifts occur, watch out! The monopoly kaleidoscope is about to turn—with results that are usually difficult to predict.

PART TWO

THE MONOPOLY RULES

Now that you understand how monopolies *really* work, you're ready to jump into the monopoly-building game yourself. In Part Two, you'll learn the Monopoly Rules—a series of vital principles used by today's most effective entrepreneurs—that can help you discover the next monopoly space, seize and retain control of that space, and stay one step ahead of the competition, even as the monopoly kaleidoscope makes its inevitable turns.

10

UNDERSTAND YOUR CURRENT MONOPOLIES

LOOK FOR THE MONOPOLY

ook for the monopoly! That's the first and the most important rule for any business. You must know *whether* your business has a monopoly, *where* the monopoly is, *why* it exists, and *when* the monopoly could end.

This is also the rule that's most often overlooked or ignored. Managers, consultants, investors, and analysts will focus intently on the company's core competencies, its strategic assets, its strong brands, its management team, or its wonderful new products. But few think to ask, "Where's the monopoly?"

I was talking about this with my friend Ken Harris, general manager of a midsized packaging company. Ken said, "Milind, I agree with you that we ought to be thinking about monopoly. My question is, How do I go about finding a monopoly? I can't just go upstairs and say to my CEO, 'We need to focus on monopoly.' I need to walk her through a *process* she can understand."

Ken had a good point. It's all very well to talk about monopolies, but how do you go about *systematically* finding one? What do you look for?

Let's start by going back to basics. *A monopoly is an ownable space for a useful period of time.* Every industry, at some point in time, will contain some profitable, ownable spaces somewhere. In new, rapidly growing industries, such spaces come along frequently. But in mature or declining industries, they are rarer.

A hundred years ago, there were several ownable spaces in the steel industry. As recently as thirty years ago, Nucor found a great one in mini-mills. But today there are probably no ownable spaces in the steel industry, and no guarantee that one will come along anytime soon. By contrast, the pharmaceutical industry still has many monopoly spaces, but their "useful period of time" (or monopoly period) may be shrinking as competition increases and price pressures heat up.

When looking for monopolies, we often forget the basic definition and fall back on false assumptions. One is the assumption that monopolies tend to be large and obvious, like Coca-Cola, Microsoft, Dell, or eBay. These industry-dominating monopolies are wonderful businesses to own, and if you spot the opportunity to seize one you'd better jump on it. But most of the real action is in thousands upon thousands of smaller and not-so-obvious monopolies. These are the profit engines that drive the vast majority of companies.

YOU HAVE A MONOPOLY WHEN . . .

To start the process, ask yourself, "Where is our current monopoly?"

(As an aside, the exact wording of this question really matters. Early in my research I made the mistake of asking an executive group, "What is your company's monopoly?" The CEO immediately said, "Oh, that's obvious. It's our brand. That's what made us what we are today." This proved to be a conversation stopper! No matter what I did or said, the group wasn't about to contradict their boss and say that, perhaps, their monopoly was based on something else. Since the key to monopoly thinking is the ability to recognize a profitable ownable space before anyone else, it's better to focus first on *where* your monopoly is.)

To locate your current monopoly, look over your entire business and find out which products, segments, or business lines pass the *five monopoly tests*. The answers to these questions can help you determine whether you have a real, live, lucrative monopoly on your hands.

The first test is: *Do your customers see only you?* We don't mean this literally. We just mean that your customers think and act as if your product or service is their only real option.

Jim Coates writes a regular technology column in the *Chicago Tribune*. It tends to be filled with heartrending stories of people having trouble with their Windows PCs—system crashes, destructive viruses, data loss, and the like.

Yet never once does anyone say that they're going to switch to a Macintosh, despite the fact that Macs have a far better track record for user-friendliness than Windows-based computers. The Windows force field is so powerful that the vast majority of computer users don't even see the Apple system as a viable alternative. That's one reason we use the word "monopoly" to describe Windows.

In a similar way, the Enterprise Rent-A-Car customer rarely, if ever, thinks about Hertz or Avis or any of the others as alternatives. In the beginning, this is precisely because the others aren't viable alternatives for the person who needs a replacement car. They won't pick her up and drop her off, they have no idea how to deal with her insurance company, and they're not conveniently located. Over time, this becomes a reflex that says, "If I need a replacement car, I call Enterprise."

The second test: *Are you invisible to your competitors?* In my research, I was amazed to find that competitors repeatedly ignored, overlooked, or dismissed monopolies right in their own backyards. We've already mentioned some of the examples, while others are familiar from recent business history. Folgers and Maxwell House ignored Starbucks; Motorola turned a blind eye to Nokia's gains in the American cell phone market; Sears was oblivious to the threat of Wal-Mart.

Why does this happen? A combination of factors, including sheer complacency and a failure to recognize the importance of shifts in the underlying economic and demographic realities.

Most crucial, perhaps, is a reliance on imaginary lines between markets, lines that are ultimately meaningless. Competitors may think of you, if at all, as a player in a different segment or industry. As a former chairman of Sears once told me, "Wal-Mart is a discounter, we're a department store. So you can't compare us to Wal-Mart." That's fine—until Wal-Mart quietly takes away all your customers.

Similarly, American Express didn't view Citibank's Visa Gold as competition: "Visa is a credit card. They extend loans to middle- and lower-income people and make money on the interest charges. We're a travel and entertainment charge card; we don't extend credit, and our customers are in the top fifteen percent of households." One day, AmEx woke up to discover that this "noncompetitive" company had eaten away at their business base, just like a "real" competitor.

In many cases suppliers, financial analysts, and other outsiders reinforce this blind spot by using the same flawed industry boundaries. But for the fortunate, overlooked company, the lesson is clear: When you find yourself in a situation where the companies you compete with seem to be unaware of your presence, you may well have a monopoly opportunity.

The third test: *Are your true competitors outside the dotted lines?* By definition, a monopoly has no effective competition within its chosen market. But this doesn't mean that if you own a monopoly, you have market dominance locked up forever. Instead, it means that your real competitors are *not* the usual suspects—fellow players in your industry as conventionally defined. Instead, they are substitutes—entirely new products, services, delivery methods, or business models—that could provide customers with the same benefits you provide in a completely different way.

Thus, Blockbuster's near-monopoly of the movie rental business is reflected in the fact that its main competitors are not other storefront outlets for tapes and DVDs but direct-mail sources like Netflix, video-on-demand programs offered by cable and satellite companies, and, ultimately, systems for downloading movies over the Internet.

In the same way, Southwest Airlines considers its real competition to be Greyhound and automobiles, since the Southwest customer rarely considers traveling on a major airline. Instead, the question in her mind is "Should I drive, take the bus, or fly Southwest?" And Howard Schultz of Starbucks spends very little time thinking about Caribou Coffee or Dunkin' Donuts. He's more worried about substitutes, alternative uses for Starbucks customers' coffee money. That's one reason Starbucks introduced herbal teas and other noncoffee beverages.

The last two tests are based in economics.

The fourth test: *Do you price like a monopolist?* And the fifth test is related to it: *Do you earn unusually high profits, "monopoly rents"?* After all, what's the point of having a monopoly if you can't set prices and earn profits like a monopolist?

This doesn't mean you ignore how customers react to prices. After all, even a classic Economics 101 monopoly like OPEC recognizes that, sooner or later, demand (and therefore total revenue) drops when prices go too high. But within those limits, a monopoly can price without worrying about competition.

So long as Honda had its minivan monopoly on the fold-down seat, it didn't do promotions or offer rebates on the Odyssey. Instead, Honda concentrated on adding production capacity to make sure that the waiting line for Odysseys wasn't too long. Honda's real worry was that dealers would overcharge customers through "premiums" and other little tricks, thereby damaging the Honda brand.

In the same way, Starbucks doesn't look over its shoulder to see what Dunkin' Donuts or Caribou Coffee are charging when it sets the price of a tall latte; the only question is "Will our revenue increase overall?" Nor does Enterprise Rent-A-Car worry about how Hertz and Avis are setting their prices; instead, it prices according to the particular neighborhood in which a rental office is located.

By contrast, if you *don't* have a monopoly, you need to constantly monitor the competition and change prices whenever the wind shifts. Just look at the price wars that periodically roil the highly competitive airline industry—with the conspicuous exception of Southwest, of course.

As a result of their exemption from price competition, monopolies are very profitable. How profitable? Three, four, five, even ten times more profitable than the all-industry average of 4.7 percent of sales. Just consider: Microsoft makes forty cents' profit on every dollar of revenue it takes in. Patented drugs like Prilosec and Lipitor throw off billions in profits every year; the pharmaceutical industry, on average, returns twenty-four cents' profit on every dollar of revenue. Coca-Cola's concentrate business returns over 35 percent on its investment, while H&R Block's tax preparation monopoly generates 30 percent profit on every dollar of revenue.*

The only monopolies that lose money are state-owned monopolies, where profits leak out through price and policy regulation, excessively high salaries, inflated payrolls, wasteful spending on pet projects, and, sometimes, corruption.

Profitability is the ultimate litmus test of monopoly. As you search for your current monopolies, watch the profit meter closely. And remember that your monopoly may be hidden inside a larger business or product line that, as a whole, shows only average profits or even losses. When you peel apart the numbers, you may find a nice, luscious small-to-medium-sized monopoly that's carrying the freight for everything else.

For example, Salton is a $1 billion firm that designs and markets small consumer appliances under a variety of well-known, specialty brands, including Breadman, Melitta, Russell Hobbs, Stiffel, Timex, and Westclox. Overall, the company is struggling: Profits are sliding, channels are squeezing margins, and competition is brutal. But buried inside

---

* Anita McGahan, "Selected Profitability Data on U.S. Industries and Companies" (Harvard Business School Note 9–792–066, February 26, 1992) is the source of the data in this paragraph. It compares ROS, ROE, and ROA across a number of different industries over a period of more than twenty years.

Salton is a wonderful little monopoly that's throwing off more profits than all the other brands combined—George Foreman indoor electric grills, which enable you to grill indoors without the fuss, smoke, and mess of outdoor grills. They are unique; no one else makes anything like them. The George Foreman grills single-handedly support the rest of the Salton line.

YOU *CAN* LEAVE HOME WITHOUT IT!

Okay. Now that you know *where* your current monopoly is, let's consider *why* it exists.

Understanding the source of your monopoly is essential to managing it properly. Consider the Honda situation again. If Honda's managers had surmised (as many people did) that their success in the minivan business was due mainly to its brand (rather than to its unique asset, the fold-down seat), the Odyssey should command premium prices even after the competition introduced the same kind of seat. That didn't happen. When competitors introduced fold-flat seats in 2004, Honda's monopoly dissipated, and the brand premium couldn't make up the difference. Honda had to start *competing,* as opposed to exploiting its monopoly.

From the mid-1950s to the late 1980s, virtually everyone in business had his or her own American Express card. There were no realistic alternatives for the business traveler in search of a convenient way to handle expenses. Carrying cash was risky, travelers' checks were cumbersome, and credit cards had very low charge limits, usually under $500. Consequently, the AmEx card was absolutely essential.

If you had asked the managers at AmEx why they were so successful, their immediate response would have been, "It's our brand. Everyone is so eager to be part of the AmEx brand that we have people begging to carry our card."

The AmEx brand did have broad appeal. But the source of American Express's monopoly was quite different. It lay in the fact that state usury laws effectively kept MasterCard and Visa out of the business travel segment until the early 1980s. In those days it was illegal to charge interest greater than 12 percent (even less in some states) on unsecured consumer loans over $500. The credit card companies were paying more than that for their working capital. Consequently, they weren't about to go after business travelers who might carry balances of thousands of dollars.

The usury laws didn't affect American Express because it was a charge card company, not a lender. For this reason Amex enjoyed a monopoly on the business travel market.

But once the states began repealing their usury laws, AmEx's monopoly disappeared. Visa and MasterCard quickly raised their credit balance limits to the point where their cards became a viable alternative for the business traveler. Suddenly AmEx looked to consumers like any other card issuer—except that you had to pay a high annual membership fee and pay your balance in full every month. People by the tens of thousands started replacing their AmEx charge cards with Visa or MasterCard.

For several years AmEx kept pushing their once-proud brand in an increasingly desperate struggle to regain their monopoly. They tried many remedies—advertising campaigns, promotions and tie-ins, even a Visa-like credit card (the Optima card)—all to no avail. The problem was that the company leadership had completely misunderstood the nature of its own monopoly. It wasn't an asset monopoly based on the power of the brand; it was a situational monopoly based on the special circumstances created by the usury laws. When the situation changed, the monopoly died.

Or consider Apple Computer's music monopoly. Apple enjoys a very large share of online music sales, thanks to its iTunes Music Store and its iPod portable music player. But what's the source of Apple's monopoly? Is it the iPod's ease of use? Is it the fact that Apple has been able to sign up all the major record labels for online music distribution? Is it the functionality of iTunes? Is it the tribal loyalty of Apple fanatics?

Here's why the answer is so important. If it's a product monopoly based on the features of the iPod, Apple must move quickly to exploit it. Sooner or later, Sony, Panasonic, Samsung, or someone else will come up with a comparable or better product, and Apple's monopoly will be over. To avert this, Apple must innovate feverishly to keep iPod's features and functions ahead of the competition.

If Apple's music monopoly is purely brand-based, then the game is already over. Once the majority of the Apple loyalists have purchased an iPod, Apple has nowhere else to go. Apple's music monopoly, like its computer monopoly, will never grow beyond four or five percent of the total market.

But what if the monopoly is more complex? What if the real monopoly is based on the total system—the combination of the iPod, the iTunes Music Store, the Apple brand, and the fact that the record labels are more willing to work with Apple than with a more aggressive competitor like Microsoft? Then Apple's monopoly has real legs. It could last for years, reach a market much larger than the number of Apple loyalists, and reap huge profits. Competitors attacking this monopoly piecemeal, through improved music players (Sony, Roxio's Nitro), online music programs (Napster reborn, Matchplay), or software (RealPlayer, Microsoft) will have less impact.

HOW LONG WILL THE MONOPOLY LAST?

This logically leads to the next question: How long is your "useful period of time" (i.e., your monopoly period) likely to be?

For an asset-based monopoly like Honda's minivan, the answer is usually straightforward: The monopoly will last exactly as long as it takes someone to copy the key asset. After Nissan, Ford, and other carmakers offered fold-flat seats in the 2004 model year, Honda's monopoly died.

By contrast, the monopoly enjoyed by income tax preparation specialist H&R Block has had a long run—over forty years. To understand why, and to define the possible expiration date on the Block monopoly, we need to analyze its source.

Every year, over 19 million American households use H&R Block to do their taxes, file their returns, and, in some cases, get advances on their expected refunds. Probably 60 percent to 70 percent of the company's clientele use H&R Block *every single year* to do their tax returns. The customers in this monopoly space are a mixed group. They include older people who are confused by the regulations and rules established by the Internal Revenue Service (IRS), recent immigrants who want to be certain they don't miss anything, and people with moderate incomes and moderately complicated tax situations. These customers stick with H&R Block either because they don't know where else to go, they're afraid that a local tax preparer (usually a certified public accountant) would cost too much, or they don't know any CPAs they trust.

What created the H&R Block monopoly? Believe it or not, the IRS! To quote the official H&R Block history:

> Until the mid-1950s, the Internal Revenue Service had actually filled out tax returns at no charge for anyone who went to their local IRS office. However, errors were common, and taxpayers' complaints led to the elimination of the service. The Bloch brothers' [the family name, changed to Block in the company name] first ad appeared at the same time that Kansas Citians were discovering the IRS would no longer prepare their tax returns.*

* From the H&R Block Company Web site: www.hrblock.com/ presscenter/pressreleases/pressRelease.jsp?PRESS_RELEASE_ ID-1263.

Within weeks, the Blochs were doing more business than their accounting practice had generated over several years. In 1956, when the IRS dropped its taxpayer service in New York City, H&R Block opened seven offices there. In time, H&R Block created franchises across the country. The company went public in 1962 and moved to the New York Stock Exchange in 1969.

Why didn't someone else copy H&R Block? One reason was that Block seized all the ownable space before anybody else could enter and compete. But it was also because the local accounting firms—Block's logical competitors—didn't see them as competitors. To a typical accounting firm, doing taxes was (and still is) a distraction. (Even Henry and Richard Bloch had decided to stop offering tax preparation services shortly before the 1955 tax season!) The work is seasonal and middle-class people just aren't willing to pay a typical CPA's rates. No wonder that CPAs didn't see Block as competition.

As a result, H&R Block has had the field to itself. Jackson Hewitt, the first significant national competitor, didn't start franchising until 1986 and remains far smaller than Block. The only other threat comes from computer tax preparation software like Intuit's TurboTax. (Remember what I said earlier: Monopolists worry about substitutes.) Meanwhile Block's revenues keep climbing steadily.

H&R Block is a great example of why situational monopolies are often more durable than asset monopolies. You can copy a fold-down seat, a manufacturing process, a new technology. How do you duplicate H&R Block's situational monopoly—or Starbucks' or Enterprise Rent-A-Car's? It wouldn't suffice to replicate the tax preparation services or coffees or rental cars; you'd have to make them available across the entire United States to even *launch* an assault on the existing monopoly.

So what *could* end H&R Block's monopoly? Essentially, a turn of the kaleidoscope creating an opportunity for a new entrant, probably someone from an entirely different business category—out of left field, as the saying goes. Some of the trends that could move the kaleidoscope are already happening. Industry dynamics are changing: Thanks to the Internet, tax data can be shipped overseas where a trained accountant can prepare a tax return at a fraction of the cost in the United States. Customer dynamics are also changing: As the baby boomers move toward retirement, the complexity of their tax returns are changing along with the specific kinds of financial advice and guidance they need.

The culminating shift could very well be the current profit squeeze on mutual funds and brokerage houses. A company like Charles Schwab or Vanguard could decide to offer tax preparation services to their best customers along with management of their 401(k)s and retirement accounts. When you're netting only $150 to $400 per account for managing funds, an additional $50 to $100 for filling out tax forms would be very welcome—especially if you already have access to the customers (and much of their financial data) and enjoy ultralow costs thanks to offshore accounting.

If this happens, H&R Block's monopoly is over.

I hope the folks who run H&R Block have performed a similar analysis and are prepared with one or more countermoves. It's a vivid example of why the first rule for would-be monopoly managers is to find and understand the nature of their current monopolies.

11

DEFEND YOUR CURRENT MONOPOLIES

HOW THE WEST WAS LOST

Never surrender a monopoly. Maybe that sounds like saying, "Don't give away a winning lottery ticket!" Who in their right minds would surrender a monopoly—just give it up?

Lots of managers do just that. Business history offers case after case of companies willingly, even wantonly, surrendering lucrative monopolies.

I first drove a Lexus in the winter of 1989. When I arrived at the San Jose airport to visit my friend Nagesh Mhatre, he picked me up in his new Lexus LS 400.

As I got in, Nagesh asked, "What do you think?" I looked around appreciatively. The Lexus had nice leather seats, a very spacious cabin, a great-sounding CD system, and a very smooth ride. "Feels just like my Mercedes-Benz," I replied. "How does it handle?"

"Why don't you drive it and see for yourself?" said Nagesh. So we switched seats. The drive took us over a stretch of Interstate 280 and then the three winding miles over back roads to Nagesh's house in Los Altos Hills. The car was steady as a rock, whether I was doing sixty-five on the freeway or sliding through tight turns at thirty-five.

"Great car!" I said to Nagesh as we got out. "Handles just like my S-Class. How did you decide to buy it?"

Nagesh smiled and said, "I was looking for a new car and walked into the Lexus dealership. They gave me the keys and said, 'Why don't you take this car away for the weekend?' Just like that! I drove it all weekend, and bought it on Monday."

"If you don't mind my asking, how much did it cost?"

"That's the best thing of all," replied Nagesh. "I was all set to pay over fifty thousand dollars for a new Mercedes. But the Lexus cost me only thirty-eight five. It's the first time I've *saved* money while buying a luxury car!"

By sheer chance, two weeks later I was talking with a friend I'll call Hans who happens to be a Mercedes executive based in New Jersey. I mentioned that I'd recently driven a Lexus. "What did you think?" Hans asked.

"Frankly," I replied, "I was impressed. It felt like my S-Class, handled like my S-Class, and had a better stereo than my S-Class. In your shoes, I'd be worried. The Lexus is like an S-Class, but it costs twenty-five percent less."

Hans was unruffled. "It's a nice car," he allowed, "but at bottom, it's just a Toyota. Once the hype dies down, the customers will come right back to Mercedes.

"As to being like your S-Class," Hans went on, "I disagree. The S-Class is bigger and has more performance. After all, it's designed to be driven on the Autobahn at a hundred and twenty miles an hour. Can you see yourself driving a Lexus at that speed?"

Before I had a chance to reply, Hans continued, "The right car to compare it to is our E-Class Mercedes. The E-Class costs only five thousand more than a Lexus, and customers will gladly pay that premium for Mercedes quality and Mercedes prestige."

Our conversation moved on to other topics, but I remember thinking, "The people at Mercedes are in deep denial. I wish Lexus was a stock. I'd make a killing."

Sure enough, the word about the new Lexus quickly spread among American auto buyers. Luxury car sales in the state of California, for example, had been dominated by Mercedes-Benz since the early 1970s. In 1988, Lexus entered the market. By 1993, Lexus was the leader on the West Coast and repeating its performance elsewhere in the United States. Mercedes had lost its luxury car monopoly.

The strangest part of the story is the fact that Mercedes surrendered its monopoly without firing a single shot in return. In fact, Mercedes behaved almost as if it *wanted* Lexus to take over the market.

At first, Mercedes shrugged off the Lexus challenge, as reflected in the comments of my friend Hans. In 1992, Mercedes introduced a new series of S-Class cars. Unfortunately, the cars were less stylish (even the normally worshipful German automotive press was unimpressed), heavier, and less reliable. At the same time, Mercedes raised the price by another $10,000. Now you could almost buy *two* Lexuses for the price of one Mercedes.

Not surprisingly, Lexus promptly raised *its* price by $7,000 and still sold every car it could make. By the time Mercedes introduced a redesigned, repriced S-Class in 1993, it was too late; Lexus was the leader and Mercedes' monopoly was history.

WHY COMPANIES SURRENDER MONOPOLIES

What prevents a great company like Mercedes from responding effectively to a threat like the one posed by Lexus?

In some cases, of course, the obvious profitability of a monopoly simply attracts competitive attention; sooner or later, other players recognize the monopoly and decide they want in on the action. If the monopoly is based primarily on product uniqueness, it may be vulnerable to imitation. That's one aspect of what happened to Mercedes—the Lexus LS 400 was a Mercedes clone at a lower price, a difficult combination to counter.

Sometimes a monopoly collapses because its managers misunderstand the nature of their business, attributing their success to the wrong factors. That's what happened to American Express, whose leaders failed to recognize that the competitive barriers created by state usury laws were a more important factor in their monopoly than the power of their vaunted brand.

Sometimes a monopoly becomes unsustainable because of profound shifts in the dynamics of the industry, the competition, and consumer behavior. As we saw in an earlier chapter, it's hard to see how the big three TV networks could have maintained their stranglehold on televised news for very long once the new technologies of cable and satellite emerged, along with the changes in consumer behavior that demanded news availability more often than once a day. But sometimes those shifts could be navigable, if only corporate managers were willing to change strategies as demanded by changing times.

In 1967, Raytheon purchased Amana as a vehicle for commercializing its new microwave oven technology. The move worked brilliantly. By the early 1970s, Amana's Radarange brand virtually owned the category, with over two-thirds of the American market for microwave ovens. But by 1976, Amana had slipped to less than one-fifth of the market, and by 1980, it was a nonentity. What happened?

The problem had nothing to do with product quality or brand image. Amana had the best ovens and a highly respected brand. Unfortunately, Amana had the *worst* management in one crucial area. In the 1970s, retail channels for appliances were changing. Consumers were moving away from traditional appliance dealers in favor of department stores and mass merchandisers. But Amana's president, George Foerstner, refused to sell the Radarange through department stores. As he put it, "I can't see how a minimum wage clerk at Penney's or Ward's can adequately display and sell this appliance."

Foerstner's insistence that customers buy from his dealers sharply restricted the visibility of the Radarange brand even as the microwave market was exploding. It also kept the prices of Amana microwaves artificially high, further depressing sales. In effect, the shortsightedness of George Foerstner and the rest of Amana's leadership team cost the company its monopoly.

Today, Sun Microsystems seems to be repeating these same mistakes. Sun shot to the top of the server market by providing engineers with a cheap, high-powered computer built around the Unix operating system. (In fact, Sun's name is an acronym for "Stanford Unix Network.") In the process, Sun undercut Digital Equipment, IBM, and other minicomputer makers. When the Internet and e-commerce exploded in the 1990s, Sun's servers were indispensable to keeping the electronic traffic moving.

However, when high-tech was hit by the "open systems" wave, led by the open-source (i.e., free) operating system called Linux, Sun refused to adapt. Rather than using standard chips from Intel or IBM and switching to Linux's open software model, Sun insisted on its own custom chips and its proprietary version of Unix. Meanwhile, IBM and Hewlett-Packard were biting off chunks of Sun's monopoly at the upper end. More recently, Dell Computer has started grabbing share at the low end. Sun can kiss its monopoly good-bye.

Sometimes a company that enjoys a monopoly finds the allure of other opportunities impossible to resist. Unfortunately, taking its eye off the ball may cost the company its monopoly. It's a problem to which premium brands are especially prone, since the temptation to pursue higher-volume (though less profitable) markets is always present.

From the 1940s through the 1960s, Cadillac represented the "top of the line," the ultimate in mass-produced American cars. It owned the lion's share of the American luxury car market; the nearest competitor, Ford's Lincoln, was far behind, and European luxury makers like Mercedes-Benz, Rolls-Royce, and Jaguar were a minor factor, popular only among a few wealthy eccentrics on either coast. The Cadillac icon even transcended cars; people eager to praise a particular product were apt to describe it as "the Cadillac of its category."

But in the early 1970s, Cadillac started to pursue volume. Between 1966 and 1978, Cadillac's annual sales volume grew from just over two hundred thousand cars to over three hundred and fifty thousand cars. But even as it grew volume, Cadillac took its eyes off its core market, affluent car buyers. It stopped innovating and started compromising its standards in the pursuit of the so-called aspirational buyer, someone whose lifelong dream had always been to own a Cadillac but who couldn't quite afford one.

Meanwhile, Mercedes was taking over the true luxury position with a well-made, tightly engineered car that handled beautifully, was reliable, and appealed to the younger generation, which was increasingly thinking of Cadillac as an old man's car. By 1980, Cadillac had lost its monopoly.

Today, Pella Windows appears to be repeating Cadillac's mistake. Traditionally, Pella used to be known as "the Cadillac of windows," with its own distribution and installation network, and outstanding quality that justified premium pricing. Recently, however, Pella's management has decided to pursue volume with the avowed aim of filling up factory capacity. As they chase larger-volume markets like the big-box retailers (Home Depot, Lowe's) and produce lower-quality lines of plastic doors and windows, Pella is voluntarily sacrificing its monopoly on the top-of-the-line market.

Finally, a monopoly sometimes collapses due to corporate complacency bordering on arrogance. The longer a company has owned a particular market or segment, the more likely it will ignore the danger signs that indicate the vulnerability of that control. The company's managers often refuse to accept the need for change, obstinately insisting that their strategies will prevail and denouncing the "ignorance" and "negativity" of their critics.

For most of the first half of the twentieth century, the Leica Rangefinder was *the* 35mm camera for professional photographers. Rugged, reliable, compact, and portable, the Rangefinder was regarded by many a professional news photographer as his best friend.

Yet during the 1950s, Leica refused to develop one of the newly popular single-lens reflex (SLR) cameras, despite possessing all the necessary technologies. Leica's thinking was, "You don't need the SLR. The Rangefinder is better, more compact, and more reliable. Why would you want to bother with the additional complications of an SLR?" Into the breach stepped Nikon, which gave all the leading professional photographers a free or steeply discounted Nikon F SLR shortly after its release in 1959. Once the pros got their hands on the Nikon F and saw that it was just as reliable as the Rangefinder and gave them more control over their images, Leica's monopoly in the professional 35mm camera market was history.

HOW TO AVOID SURRENDERING YOUR MONOPOLIES

In this chapter, we've recounted quite a collection of horror stories about once-great monopolies that were needlessly squandered by their owners. What lessons can we learn about how to protect any monopoly you may be lucky enough to own? Here are five.

1. *Don't sneer at potential competition—especially from an unexpected source.* As we've seen, many companies have been blindsided by substitute suppliers emerging out of left field to steal their markets. Be prepared at any moment to defend against your competition by upgrading your product or service, adding new features, or finding new applications or markets.

2. *Be certain you understand the true nature and sources of your monopoly.* Don't mindlessly repeat the favored mantra describing the key to your company's success— "It's our brand," "It's our product," or "It's our quality." Chances are excellent that it may be wrong—and that the next monopolist in your industry may be waiting for an opportunity to knock the props out from under the *real* source of your monopoly advantage.

3. *Be ready to shift along with industry, competitor, and customer dynamics.* Remember that the monopoly kaleidoscope can turn at any time. Keep track of changes in your environment (even changes that may appear insignificant at first glance), and think about how these changes might interact and snowball to devastating effect.

4. *Keep your eye on the monopoly ball.* There's nothing wrong with trying to expand into new markets, so long as these efforts don't distract you from protecting your precious monopoly. In particular, don't rush to grow your sales volume without first considering the potential impact of broader demographics on your brand image. To update the old adage, sometimes the wisest course is to put all your eggs in one basket, and then *watch that basket.*

5. *Don't be complacent.* Nothing breeds failure like too much success, enjoyed too easily, for too long a time. Be on the lookout for signs of arrogance in your corporate culture; like the social and moral decadence that eventually destroyed Imperial Rome, these are early indications that your empire is ripe for takeover by the barbarians.

The price of monopoly is eternal vigilance.

12

DISCOVER
THE NEXT MONOPOLY

CHANCE FAVORS ONLY THE PREPARED MIND

Monopolies are elusive. They are also fluid, changing rapidly right in front of our eyes. What's more, there are no flashing signs, no blinking neon lights, no welcoming bells that say, "Nice monopoly, enter here!" Most often, people discover monopoly spaces by stumbling across them while they're searching for something else. When that happens, they probably feel a bit like "stout Cortez" in the famous poem by John Keats:*

> . . . *when with eagle eyes*
> *He star'd at the Pacific—and all his men*
> *Look'd at each other with a wild surmise—*
> *Silent, upon a peak in Darien.*

(Never mind that Keats is guilty of one of the famous literary boners; the Pacific Ocean was discovered by Balboa, not "stout Cortez"! He still wrote a great poem.)

---

* John Keats (1795–1821), "On First Looking into Chapman's Homer."

Successful entrepreneurs and successful companies are *always* thinking about their next monopolies. Part of this may be paranoia, the fear that they will miss out on the next big thing, the next big opportunity, and become commoditized. More fundamentally, it is because finding the next monopoly is like finding the next big oil field; there are no guarantees, and luck plays a role along with talent. Fortunately, the words of scientist Louis Pasteur are true here: "Chance favors only the prepared mind." If you know what you're looking for and have some ideas about where to look, you can be poised to anticipate when a new ownable space will open up and be the first to capitalize on it. But you have to be ready.

LOOK FOR THE PATTERN

So what can you do to discover your company's next monopoly space—not by serendipity, but by design? What you should be looking for is a *pattern,* a *situation* where customers want *something*—a nice tasting cup of coffee, a convenient replacement car—that existing players can't or won't provide, and that you can now provide better, cheaper, or more effectively. Specifically, you are looking for situations where the following three conditions coexist:

1. *An emerging need.* First, you want to find a significant group of customer wants or needs—something that isn't being provided adequately or at all today.

2. *Incumbent inertia.* Companies currently serving this group of customers are unable or unwilling to provide that "something" efficiently or cost-effectively.

3. *New capability.* You can envision new ways of meeting these needs profitably, yet at a price that customers will be ready to pay.

At any moment, the business universe contains hundreds of situations in which one or two of these conditions exist. That's not good enough; all three must come together. When they do, a monopoly space is opening up.

Case in point: CNN's "all-news monopoly" came about *precisely* because a large group of busy people wanted news on *their* time schedule (emerging need), while CBS, NBC, and ABC were reluctant to change their existing news pattern because in their view news didn't make money (incumbent inertia), and satellite and cable made it easier to find and serve these all-news customers and still make a profit (new capability). If any one of these three factors hadn't been in place, there would have been no monopoly and probably no CNN!

UNDERSTAND THE CORE BELIEF

One way to begin scouting for monopoly opportunities is by analyzing the current monopolies in and around your industry. This involves defining the current monopoly's core belief; examining how the dynamics around the monopoly are changing; and identifying the changes that will destroy the current monopoly and create new ones.

First, what do we mean by a *core belief?*

Every industry and every successful monopoly rests on a core belief. The core belief may reflect a particular view of customers and their behavior. For example, the traditional car rental industry once monopolized by Hertz was based on the core belief "People rent cars when they travel." Starting from this premise, Hertz built a successful business around hundreds of airport locations and an array of services designed to cater specifically to the travel market. (Note that this core belief implies that people rent cars *only* when they travel.)

A core belief may reflect a set of assumptions about what it takes to succeed in a particular industry. For example, the major airlines share the core belief "A hub-and-spoke system is essential for competing efficiently to transport travelers to a broad range of destinations."

A core belief may define the perceived role of the companies in a particular industry. For example, the traditional coffee makers like Maxwell House and Folgers shared the core belief "Our job is to sell ground coffee in cans in supermarkets."

Or a core belief may embody an industry's value system. For decades, American automakers operated on the basis of such core beliefs as "There's no profit in small cars," "An auto purchase needs to include prolonged haggling between the buyer and the dealer," and "The only *real* cars are those powered by gas-fueled internal-combustion engines."

The more successful a monopoly—the longer it lasts and the greater its profits—the more deeply entrenched its core beliefs become. You can see the danger in this for as we know, the world never stops changing. At some point, the core belief stops reflecting underlying economic realities. But the entire industry, now thoroughly wedded to the core belief, pushes forward blindly, unquestioningly.

Therefore, when you're trying to find a new monopoly opportunity in a particular industry, analyzing the industry's core belief is a good place to start. This exercise can bring insights that reveal the industry's blind spots, and the forces or trends that might make its core belief—and the existing monopoly based on it—obsolete.

If your core belief is that the coffee industry is synonymous with "coffee in cans on the supermarket shelf," you won't be ready when customers start buying their coffee in expensive single portions from chichi corner outlets. Similarly, if your core belief is that there's no profit in small cars, you'll never put your heart into designing one and marketing it aggressively.

IDENTIFY THE TIDAL FORCES

Once you've identified the core belief around which your industry is organized, the next step is to begin searching for emerging changes in industry, customer, and competitor dynamics. Increasingly, these changes are driven by powerful tidal forces that can revolutionize an industry—and destroy an existing monopoly—overnight. If you can spot one of these tidal forces before the other players recognize it, you have a chance of creating a highly profitable new monopoly.

Here's a current example. The American auto industry enjoys a near-monopoly in the highly profitable SUV marketplace. This monopoly is based on an interlocking set of core beliefs, including: "Americans love to drive big cars," "American drivers will always enjoy relatively low fuel costs," and "American voters will always insist on loose government regulation of their big cars." (In regard to this last belief, as you probably know, current federal regulations categorize SUVs as "light trucks," which exempts these vehicles from the fuel economy requirements that apply to other passenger cars.)

Is there any tidal force in today's environment that could shatter one or more of these core beliefs?

One such force relates to gasoline supplies and prices. As the middle class population in China and India grows, auto sales in those countries are skyrocketing. As a result, drivers in India and China will soon be buying a larger share of the world's oil production. In turn, sooner or later, oil prices must go up, even in the United States. When this happens, how will this affect the attitude of Americans toward their fuel-guzzling SUVs? Will environmentalists force Congress to adopt more stringent fuel-efficiency standards? Will drivers, stung by price shock at the gas pump, switch to more fuel-efficient (i.e., Japanese) SUVs? Or will they dump SUVs altogether?

Another tidal wave that's currently gathering force is the

exporting of white-collar professional jobs from the United States to countries like Eastern Europe, Russia, and India, where highly skilled professional talent is available at a fraction of the domestic cost. Thanks to the Internet, it's now practical to transmit expertise across borders and oceans more quickly and easily than ever before.

We've already discussed the potential impact of this trend on a company like H&R Block. What will happen to its monopoly on tax preparation if Charles Schwab starts offering low-cost, or even free tax preparation advice from accountants overseas? But more broadly, how might the new availability of cheap, international white-collar expertise eventually shatter the monopolies enjoyed by such powerful American institutions as the major accounting firms, consultancies, think tanks, universities, advertising agencies, and publishers? This is a question that strategists at organizations like Ernst & Young, McKinsey & Company, the Rand Corporation, Stanford University, Young & Rubicam, and Random House ought to be grappling with—today.

THINK LIKE AN ENTRANT

Once you identify the major tidal forces with the potential to destroy the current monopoly, start thinking like a new entrant, someone completely outside of a particular industry. Imagine one of today's smartest competitors—someone like Michael Dell (Dell Computer), Steve Jobs (Apple), Bill Gates (Microsoft), David Neeleman (JetBlue Airways), Richard

Branson (Virgin), or Howard Schultz (Starbucks)—eyeing your industry. Ask yourself, "Where would a smart new entrant attack? Where would he focus, and why?"

One mental trick that can help you answer this question is to turn the core belief upside down. Unconstrained by conventional wisdom or past investments, a new entrant is in a position to behave like the proverbial "man from Mars," questioning assumptions that people inside the monopoly take for granted.

For example, the core belief in the mainstream credit card industry can be summarized as "medium deadbeats." Translation: We make our money from people who run up balances and pay them off over two to six months (but not before racking up handsome interest charges). Naturally, the card issuers lose money on the *true* deadbeats, consumers who run up balances and then can't—or won't—pay them at all. They also lose money on customers who pay their charge bills in full every month. If a customer charges $200 in purchases every month and pays the bill promptly, the credit card company receives only $1.40 in merchant fees on that customer. It costs an average of $1.57 just to send out a monthly bill to the cardholder. The profit math simply doesn't work.

As a result, consumers who pay their credit card bills promptly are treated relatively poorly by the card companies. Many end up irritated by ever-escalating annual fees imposed by the issuers in a desperate search for profits, as well as subtle pressures to either pay faster or run up their balances.

Now examine the situation the way an imaginative new

entrant might. Remember, a monopoly opportunity exists where there is (1) an emerging need, (2) incumbent inertia, and (3) new capability. In the credit card case, the first two conditions for the monopoly pattern are already present. Credit card users who pay their bills in full every month need (and frankly deserve) low-priced, courteous service. But credit card companies can't make money on these customers without charging them large annual membership fees. Ergo: unmet need!

Just a few years ago, there might have been little or nothing that a new entrant could do to alter the situation. But today, the Internet offers an alternative approach to managing credit card accounts. A savvy new entrant could approach consumers with high credit ratings and make the following offer: "We'll give you a Visa card with a low interest rate and a nominal annual fee, provided you maintain your high credit rating, pay your bill promptly, *and* all transactions—invoices, payments, queries—are handled via the Internet. If you insist on receiving a printed invoice via snail mail, it'll cost you $2.50 per statement."

The business model would resemble that of Vanguard in mutual funds, focusing on consumers with excellent credit, charging them really low prices (e.g., $1/2\%$ per transaction) and making money by keeping marketing costs and credit write-offs extremely low. It would serve a customer segment of 25 million households who charge, on average, $3,000 per year. It could be a nice, profitable little monopoly with annual revenues of around $375 million. Not bad!

In effect, this new business model turns the industry's

core belief on its head. It replaces "We make our money from medium deadbeats" with "We make our money from prompt payers." Perhaps this new core belief will open the door to a potential new monopoly.

In much the same way, Enterprise created its monopoly by transforming the core belief "People rent cars (only) when they travel" into "People (also) rent cars when their own car is in the shop for repairs, or when they need an extra vehicle for some special purpose." Volkswagen created—and then dominated—a new niche in the American auto market by replacing the core belief "There's no profit in small cars" with "Plenty of people will buy a small car that's well built, efficient, economical, durable, and marketed with pizzazz."

Of course, there are other potential monopoly spaces within the credit card industry, other spaces that are rendered all but invisible by the industry's core belief. For example, most credit card companies shun customers at the *other* end of the credit spectrum, namely, people with poor or no credit.

This was exactly the space discovered by Shailesh Mehta, CEO of Providian Financial. He recognized two out of the three conditions of a monopoly space—a customer need (the need for credit for people with bad credit ratings), and the inability of existing players to meet this need. But how could this need be met profitably?

Providian Financial came up with the idea of *prepaid* credit cards. A prepaid card eliminated credit risk by accepting charges only up to the amount that the customer had paid in advance. And a surprisingly large number of customers were willing to pay money in advance for the privilege of spending it later. (Among other advantages, it let them avoid the danger of carrying cash if they lived or worked in a dangerous neighborhood. It also helped cardholders manage their own spending by establishing a strict monthly budget.) It was a wonderful little monopoly for Providian.

So never be satisfied with finding just one monopoly space. Examine every corner of your industry. You will often find multiple potential monopoly spaces characterized by the same pattern of customer needs, existing suppliers unable or unwilling to meet those needs, and possible new ways of meeting them.

VALIDATE YOUR INSIGHTS

Now analysis takes over. You have to buttress your intuition with facts and figures as well as a carefully calculated blend of imagination and caution.

What you want to know are three things. First, *how big is the potential monopoly space?* How many customers does it contain? What volume of revenues and profits might be possible? How long is the monopoly period likely to last?

Second, *what is keeping other companies from claiming this space?* Are they deterred by the anticipated costs of creating a new product or service, opening new offices or production facilities, or launching a marketing program? Are they worried about the danger of cannibalizing their existing business, damaging their brand image, or losing their market focus? Do they believe that the space isn't worth entering?

Finally, *can your company overcome the barriers that other competitors perceive?* If so, how? Can you develop a plausible business plan that sketches how you will create profits in a market space where other companies believe it can't be done?

During this period of analysis, maintaining objectivity is critical—and very difficult. You have to balance a healthy sense of skepticism with enthusiasm for the idea. Both qualities are important. But if either one is allowed to dominate your thinking, it may skew your analysis.

If you take away any single lesson from this book, the most important may be the one this chapter teaches: *The manager's chief responsibility is to find his company's next monopoly space.*

Is this easy to do? No. Like Balboa, you'll face some unknown risks and unpredictable challenges in your quest for business spaces no competitor has claimed. But when you experience the moment of epiphany that comes with discovering your own private Pacific, you'll know it was worth struggling for.

13

SEIZE THE MONOPOLIES IN YOUR OWN BACKYARD

THE PRICE OF MYOPIA

For twenty-five years, there were two Sears department stores on Chicago's North Shore. Both were more than ten miles inland from the affluent lakefront suburbs. In the last five years, Home Depot has put four—that's right, *four*—large stores right in or near these lakefront suburbs. In the process, these Home Depot stores have attracted thousands of upscale customers who stop in to pick up supplies they need for home improvement projects—things like lumber, nails, shelf brackets, and electrical tape. Once they're in the store, these affluent homebodies are likely to check out Depot's prices on more expensive, profitable items—things like power tools, carpeting, light fixtures, and appliances.

Things they *used* to buy at Sears.

Adding insult to injury, Sears' worldwide corporate headquarters is located—you guessed it—in Chicago's northwest suburbs! If Home Depot could see the profit potential for *four* large stores on the North Shore, why didn't Sears put in at least two new stores much earlier? What other opportunities has Sears overlooked in its own backyard?

Unfortunately, Sears isn't the only large incumbent company to ignore monopoly-building opportunities that are virtually under its nose. But the myopia of the big guys creates wonderful opportunities for the little guys, entrants who see what the incumbents miss.

In an earlier chapter, we talked about how entrepreneur David Neeleman recognized the monopoly potential in an underused terminal at New York's JFK Airport. Neeleman used this space to establish a Big Apple beachhead for upstart JetBlue Airways. It's a great story of monopoly building. But to me, the most intriguing aspect of the JetBlue saga *isn't* how JetBlue made its JFK gamble pay off. The real question is: How did Southwest Airlines miss the opportunity right in its backyard?

After all, Southwest was already flying in and out of such (relatively) nearby towns as Islip, New York; Providence, Rhode Island; and Manchester, New Hampshire. It had the brand, it had the people, and it had the planes. It even had the same entrepreneurial, opportunistic philosophy as JetBlue founder David Neeleman (who sold his earlier startup, Morris Air, to Southwest in the early 1990s). So why did Southwest pass up this billion-dollar monopoly right in its backyard?

Southwest Airlines didn't see the opportunity! Traditionally, Southwest Airlines looked for secondary airports and the host of advantages they offered: low landing fees, rapid flight turnaround, no congestion, and no head-to-head competition with major airlines. They also opted, whenever possible, for locations with few or no weather problems, many short-hop destinations (500 to 700 miles away), and no labor issues. But JFK was a primary airport with heavy traffic, (presumably) high landing fees, congestion, weather problems, labor union issues, major airlines just fifteen miles away, and few short-hop destinations. From Southwest's perspective, JFK just didn't fit.

But when it came to JFK, Southwest's ordinary yardstick was flawed. In terms of *domestic* traffic, JFK was a secondary airport. Because the airport was grossly underutilized *during the day*, airport management was motivated to negotiate lower landing fees. By 2000, access to JFK was improving: The subway was getting closer, and buses and limos would follow if traffic grew. The key, as Neeleman proved, was giving jaded, value-conscious New Yorkers a reason to fly out of JFK.

It's hard to be too critical of Southwest Airlines. Their success formula, which had worked so brilliantly for so many years, simply didn't work when applied to JFK Airport. It took David Neeleman and JetBlue to prove that a new monopoly opportunity had existed there all along.

FORD PASSES ON THE MINIVAN

Sears and Southwest have plenty of company. Time and time again, experienced managers at many of America's greatest companies keep overlooking monopoly opportunities right in their own backyards.

Ford ignored a huge monopoly opportunity for over a decade, starting in the late 1960s. At that time, Don DelaRossa, one of the company's top designers, had begun talking about "an all-purpose vehicle, neither station wagon nor van, that women as well as men could drive, a car for the suburban housewife during the week and for the family on the weekends, a sawed-off hybrid of a van and a wagon, with lots of interior room."* By 1976, Ford's own market research suggested that such a car, then termed "the Mini/max," would sell 800,000 units in its first year.

The concept was championed by a Ford executive named Norman Krandall, who had a reputation as something of a maverick. He pointed out that the new car would be profitable even if it only sold a *quarter* as many as the projected total. But his pleas fell on deaf ears:

Krandall was surprised by how little reaction there was to his research. This was a brand-new market he had uncovered, and the Ford Motor Company was supposed to react to the market. But the market, he realized, no longer mattered to most of the men running the company; they thought that they could dictate the market.†

Ford refused to build the Mini/max. Several years later, Lee Iacocca, who had left Ford and subsequently become

* David Halberstam, *The Reckoning* (New York: William Morrow & Company, 1986), 562.
† Ibid., 564.

CEO of Chrysler, decided to press ahead with it. Chrysler launched the minivan in the fall of 1983. It sold over 200,000 units in its first twelve months and helped rescue Chrysler from the brink of disaster.

As we saw in an earlier chapter, IBM and Compaq missed a huge monopoly in their backyards when they allowed Dell to capture a unique category of customers within the PC market, which they dominated—engineers who needed custom-designed computers to handle specialized technical tasks. Rather than responding to the needs of engineers like Charlie, they left the space open for Dell Computer, which is now the colossus of the PC industry. Compaq is gone (acquired by Hewlett Packard) and IBM recently announced plans to exit the category it virtually invented back in 1981.

Revlon and other traditional cosmetics companies ignored a backyard monopoly that became the basis of The Body Shop. Focusing on women who want natural, earth-friendly cosmetics that aren't tested on animals (and without resorting to expensive advertising or marketing campaigns), The Body Shop has grown into a multinational company with over $750 million in revenues and more than 1,900 outlets in fifty countries around the world.

Maybe my favorite example is Movie Gallery, founded by Joe Malugen and Harrison Parrish in Dothan, Alabama, in 1985. Today, Movie Gallery is the third largest movie retailer in the United States, with over 2,200 stores throughout North America. What's Movie Gallery's secret? Simple—they are the largest source of video and video game rental and sale in rural and secondary markets in the United States. In fact, in many small towns and villages across North America, they are the *only* video and video game rental place. That's their monopoly.

As a result, while industry leader Blockbuster has posted losses two years out of the past three, and second fiddle Hollywood Entertainment's profits are flat, Movie Gallery's revenues and profits have doubled almost every year since the mid-1990s. Since 2000, the company's stock price has risen from just over $1 per share to a high of $22.

DON'T MISS THE MAN IN THE GORILLA SUIT!

Managers often fail to spot and exploit these opportunities in their backyards because they almost literally cannot see them. They are so focused on their traditional view of the market that they suffer from what psychologists call *frame blindness*.

I got a firsthand exposure to frame blindness recently when I participated in a simple classroom experiment. Thirty-two of us were asked to watch a short videotape of two teams of students—one team in white T-shirts, one team in black—as they passed a basketball around. Before running the tape, the instructor asked us to watch carefully and count how many times the students in black passed the ball to one another.

As the tape ran, I concentrated hard. I counted fifteen passes. When the lights came up, the instructor asked for volunteers to report their results.

"Fifteen passes," one person said.

"I counted sixteen," said another.

"Seventeen," said a third. A quick vote established a consensus count of fifteen.

"Okay," said the instructor. "Now tell me, how many of you saw the man in the gorilla suit?"

We stared at him, then at one another. Man in the gorilla suit? What man? What gorilla suit? What is he talking about?

Smiling, the instructor reran the videotape. Sure enough, about a third of the way through, a man in a gorilla suit appeared on the screen. He walked among the two teams, handled the ball, and even waved at the camera before walking offstage. We'd all been so focused on counting the passes that we'd completely missed him!

If I hadn't experienced it, I'd never have believed it.

In the same fashion, business managers are often so busy studying the market as they know it (counting passes) that they completely overlook anomalies (the man in the gorilla suit) right under their noses.

How can you avoid falling victim to frame blindness? There are no foolproof preventive measures. But here are five techniques you should find useful.

1. *Question received wisdom.* The next time someone shoots down a new idea by saying, "That's not our business," or " Customers don't need that," or "There's no money in that segment of the market," don't simply nod and move on to the next topic. Instead, ask some pointed questions: "Why not? Why isn't that our business? Who

says the customers don't need it? Why is it difficult to make money in that segment? Could someone else do it? What would it take? Is somebody already doing it? Why or why not?"

2. *Don't take yes for an answer.* Most companies have particular products, markets, or customer groups they consider "successful," while others represent "a challenge." But if you regard your "successful" businesses with complacency, you may be overlooking opportunities to achieve far more. Back in the mid-1990s, when Coca-Cola CEO Roberto C. Goizueta was asked to identify markets with outstanding growth opportunities for Coke, he would often reply, "Southern California"—this at a time when the nations of the former Soviet Union, mainland China, the "tigers" of Southeast Asia, and sub-Saharan Africa were all welcoming new floods of western products. But Goizueta wasn't joking. He knew that Coke consumption rates in Southern California were actually *lower* than in such countries as Hungary or South Africa, and Goizueta wouldn't be satisfied until people everywhere were guzzling Coke as avidly as the company's most fanatical customers.

3. *Study markets adjacent to your own.* Start by drawing a map of the markets in which your company competes—not a geographic map, but a conceptual one, based on product types, customer groupings, or other relevant categories. Mark off territories controlled by all of the major players, indicating, as best you can, their relative

size. Once this map is completed, ask yourself, "What would we find if we began to explore the white space *beyond* this map? What other markets exist nearby that might be ripe for colonization?" If executives at Coca-Cola had developed such a map back in the 1970s, they would have begun by depicting the market for carbonated beverages, with territories labeled Coke, Pepsi, 7-Up, Dr. Pepper, and so on. But the extended map would have included such regions as fruit drinks, teas and coffees, bottled waters, and even, in its far reaches, snack foods like chips, tacos, and pizzas.

Of course, Coke never did focus on that broader map. Instead, some of these areas have become important growth opportunities for Coca-Cola's chief competitor, Pepsi.

Will every territory shown on your map represent a potential monopoly space? Of course not. But creating such a map will help ensure that you don't overlook any "obvious" spaces in your own (metaphorical) backyard.

4. *Rewrite your formula.* If your company has developed a proven formula for success over time, you're very lucky. Now change it! We don't mean that you should discard the formula in cases where it still works. But conversely, don't *assume* that the formula applies under new business circumstances, in new geographic settings, or under new demographic conditions. Above all, don't let a "proven formula" become an easy way of writing off an unproven new opportunity, the way Southwest wrote off the JFK opportunity because it didn't fit the company's

traditional recipe. Remember, a new approach to business *never* works—until it does.

5. *Break out of your mental routine.* Most managers have a set of six or ten or fifteen favorite metrics, tailored to their industry, that they diligently monitor—same-store sales, customer satisfaction ratings, average revenue per customer. That's fine; it's important to do a good job of counting how many times the basketball gets passed around. But it's also important to periodically break the frame and take a fresh look at your industry, from a new perspective. Invite an expert from some completely different industry to spend a week with you and discuss his observations; or, conversely, discover what you can learn by spending a week in an industry you've never worked in. And devote time in management meetings to asking "What if?" questions, the more outlandish the better.

Monopoly opportunities are rare and precious things. Don't make the all-too-common mistake of ignoring one that is right under your nose.

14

WORK BACKWARDS

BEGIN WITH THE END IN MIND

Earlier in this book, I described the concept of the sustainable competitive advantage as a sort of holy grail of business—a mythic panacea that many assume (wrongly) will guarantee success.

If any concept is even more revered than sustainable competitive advantage, it may be *strategy*. Virtually everyone in business takes it for granted that the difference between a successful company and an unsuccessful one is that one has a winning strategy, while the other—well, the other just doesn't.

There's nothing wrong with having a great strategy. I'm all for it! But the usual emphasis on strategy is misplaced. Our greatest entrepreneurs don't focus on strategy but rather on finding their next monopoly.

In effect, they work backwards! First, they figure out where they can create a monopoly, how long it might last, and how profitable it can be. Then they search for the strategy that will get them there quickly and without spending a fortune.

Monopoly is the goal; strategy is simply the road to that goal. And as business guru Stephen Covey preaches (cribbing from Aristotle), the key to success in any endeavor is to "begin with the end in mind."

The youthful Michael Dell realized that there was a mass of customers, primarily engineers, who wanted a PC customized to their requirements. He started assembling and shipping the PCs out of his college dorm room. He gradually discovered that to make money selling customized PCs, he *had* to sell direct (retailers weren't interested); he *had* to sell over the telephone (a direct sales force would be too expensive); he *had* to have an ultraflexible manufacturing setup (to make thousands of one-of-a-kind PCs); and he *had* to make suppliers carry the inventory (since he didn't have much capital).

So Dell built his strategy—the efficient supply chain, the direct ordering mechanism, and all the rest—because it was the only way he could capitalize on the monopoly space he'd discovered. He didn't first devise a strategy, then use it to discover the monopoly space.

COPYING DELL ISN'T THE SAME AS *BEING* DELL

Without Michael Dell's ownable space, copying his tactics— "benchmarking Dell," in MBA-speak—is an exercise in futility.

Consider the saga of Dell look-alike, Gateway. Dell was started in 1984 out of Michael Dell's dorm room; Gateway was started in 1985 with a $10,000 loan guaranteed by founder Ted Waitt's grandmother. Like Dell, Gateway started out selling PCs over the telephone. Like Dell, Gateway is (or tries to be) a low-cost player. Dell went public in 1989; Gateway went public in 1993.

For several years, both companies rode the PC and Internet waves. But their paths diverged dramatically in 2000. Dell kept growing, while Gateway's revenues have collapsed, dropping from $9.0 billion in 2000 to $3.4 billion in 2003.

Ted Waitt has tried everything to turn Gateway around— pursuing online sales more aggressively, opening a string of Gateway retail stores, branching into consumer electronics, and (most recently) jumping into the discount computer market through the acquisition of eMachines. Nothing is working. Gateway's stock price has dropped from a peak of nearly $100 to as low as two dollars (it currently hovers around four dollars).

There are many reasons for Gateway's decline— unfocused management, a disruptive headquarters move, tactical mistakes—but the fundamental problem is that Gateway, unlike Dell, has never had a monopoly space.

Whereas Dell was the sole supplier of customized, built-to-order PCs to engineers, scientists, and other technical workers in larger corporations, Gateway sold its PCs to smaller businesses and consumers who just wanted a low-priced computer. They didn't care about precise specifications and would buy a PC wherever the price was lowest. No wonder Gateway's market disappeared when lower-priced PCs started showing up at Best Buy and other mass retailers.

Today, still lacking an ownable space, Gateway is just another low-cost player in a viciously competitive commodity industry with razor-thin margins and prices that keep dropping. The results are painfully obvious: Since the end of the Internet boom, Gateway has lost $1.8 billion.

Working backward, from monopoly to strategy, is especially important today. Why? Because in the era of the New Competition, the familiar strategies managers counted on from the 1950s through the 1980s—strong brands, unique products, high quality, low costs—have stopped working. Now competition is global, markets are fragmented, and technologies leak out almost overnight. Those classic strategies once created monopolies. No more.

Examples are easy to find. For many packaged goods manufacturers, it's still an article of faith that a big brand supported by a large advertising budget creates brand pull that delivers monopoly-style profits. This formula worked when retailers were fragmented; they needed the brand's ability to attract customers more than the brand needed them. Today, however, over 20 percent of the sales of such packaged goods makers as Procter & Gamble, Johnson Wax, and Rubbermaid go through *one* retailer—Wal-Mart. In this situation, pulling the brand lever doesn't deliver monopoly profits. A few more sales dollars may flow into Wal-Mart, but the margins of the manufacturers still get squeezed.

In the era of the New Competition, it's increasingly difficult to keep product features proprietary. Whether it is flavors, features, or fares, companies rarely get a chance to offer customers anything unique for more than a few months. Colgate comes out with a disposable electric toothbrush; Procter & Gamble matches it within months. Miller rolls out a low-carb beer; Budweiser is quick to follow. In this environment, product differentiation lacks the monopoly power it once wielded.

Twenty years ago, Maytag had a monopoly because millions of consumers believed its washers, dryers, ranges, and dishwashers boasted better quality and reliability than other brands. Today, consumers don't see much difference among appliance brands. As a result, channel gorillas like Home Depot and Sears Brand Central are squeezing the margins enjoyed by Maytag and every other manufacturer.

Scale is another corporate asset that has lost much of its power. Thirty years ago, IBM's huge, global sales force created a highly profitable monopoly. Nobody else could match IBM's ability to market electronic equipment to everyone from the local lawyer to the federal government. Today, with the advent of online sales and service, a large sales force merely guarantees high costs. You don't need it to sell to the federal government, and you can't afford it to sell to the local lawyer. Scale no longer guarantees a monopoly.

REVLON: BIG BRAND, NO PROFITS

The story of Revlon vividly illustrates the quagmire into which a once-powerful brand can wander when managers remain focused on strategy rather than on monopoly.

Any way you look at it, Revlon is a major consumer brand. It spends heavily on advertising ($90 million in 2003 alone). It uses actresses and supermodels like Lauren Hutton, Cindy Crawford, Julianne Moore, Eva Mendes, Jaime King, and Halle Berry to promote its products in glamorous, sexy advertisements in newspapers, in magazines, on billboards, and on TV.

For decades after its founding in 1932, Revlon's focus on brand paid off. In 1940, Revlon's sales were $2.8 million. They increased sixfold in the 1940s, sevenfold in the 1950s, and threefold in the 1960s. And until the late 1980s, Revlon was incredibly profitable.

Over the last decade, however, Revlon's performance has been terrible. The company has posted losses for the last twenty-two quarters, hemorrhaged nearly $600 million since 2001, and hired three CEOs in the past four years. Revlon stock has dropped from a high of nearly $60 in 1998 to under $3. What happened?

The problem isn't lack of investment. Revlon continues to spend aggressively to promote its products. It isn't incompetent brand management. Critics of advertising agree that Revlon's recent campaigns, produced by Deutsch Advertising, a respected creative powerhouse, were stylish, sophisticated, and beautiful.

Revlon's real problem is its retailers. Revlon's focus has always been the mass market; in the words of biographer Andrew Tobias, company founder Charles Revson "injected a little excitement into . . . the 'quiet desperation' of the average housewife's daily life." Unlike upscale department-store cosmetics makers like Helena Rubinstein and Elizabeth Arden, Revlon sold its products through drugstores and other mass outlets.

But as the corner drugstores consolidated and Walgreens and Wal-Mart became Revlon's dominant customers, the company's margins got squeezed. The numbers tell the story. A department-store brand like Estée Lauder has gross margins of over 70 percent, while Revlon's margins are ten points lower. In Revlon's "masstige" category, a strong brand no longer equates with strong profits. Walgreens and Wal-Mart get the traffic, while Revlon gets stuck with the tab.

Revlon's leadership must shift its focus from "strategic" questions *(Should we reposition our brand? Should we change advertising agencies? Should we alter our production formulas so as to reduce costs?)* to the one crucial issue: *Where in our industry is there an identifiable, ownable, profitable monopoly space?*

In the same way, it's time for managers in every industry to overcome their natural tendency, reinforced by decades of B-school indoctrination and consultant-speak, to focus on strategy, and assuming that somehow a great strategy will create a great monopoly. Instead, we need to ask ourselves, "Even assuming our strategy works as we say it will (which it rarely does), *will it create a monopoly?"*

Here's my modest proposal. Cancel next year's "strategic planning" process at your corporation. Replace it with a "monopoly prospecting" exercise. Only *after* you've identified the leading candidates for your next monopoly space should you begin to consider strategies that might take you there.

After all, until you know where you're going, your chances of getting there are pretty slim.

15

FOCUS ON SPEED TO SPACE

BUILD OUT FAST—OR LOSE YOUR MONOPOLY

Finding a monopoly space isn't enough. You've got to be quick to seize it and build up a fence to keep the competition out, at least for a time. In Aesop's fable, the tortoise beat the hare, but in business "slow and steady" will generally *lose* the race. Speed to space is key! Sooner or later, competitors will charge into your space. If you aren't well dug in, there goes your monopoly.

Finding a new monopoly is a little like being the first prospector to discover gold in a particular region. Having found the initial seam, you can take time to consolidate your operations, build proper mines and collection points, and so forth. Or you can move quickly to lock up the best sites in the area before word spreads and the gold rush begins.

Sometimes you have the luxury of time. If you *know* you have a long monopoly period because of patents, unique technologies, or some other asset that competitors cannot match, you don't have to rush. You can consolidate your position and *then* lock up the rest of the market. Chester F.

Carlson's patents on dry-copy technology gave him a long monopoly period, allowing Xerox to take its time when rolling out its copiers. Pfizer controls the Lipitor monopoly until 2009, which means it can take some time in developing new applications for the drug.

Southwest Airlines enjoyed an extended monopoly period, not because of patents or technologies but because of the core belief of its mainstream industry competitors. To the managers at American, United, and Delta, Southwest was a *discount* carrier, no different from PeopleExpress and the other discounters they'd killed off in the mid-1980s. Feeling secure behind their hub-and-spoke systems, the majors disregarded Southwest, which could therefore take its own sweet time in rolling out its model across the United States.

Of course, if you assume that your monopoly barriers give you time to expand in a deliberate fashion, you run the risk of complacency. Growing fat on the monopoly profits from its historic patents, Xerox failed to capitalize on the new computing innovations being developed in its own research facility, the legendary Palo Alto Research Center (Xerox PARC). Xerox soon lost its monopoly to upstarts like Canon, Ricoh, and (unkindest cut of all) Fuji, its former Japanese licensee.

Today, with the number of discount airlines increasing, Southwest is in a bind. If it slows down its nationwide expansion, it risks losing potentially lucrative markets to new players like JetBlue, ATA, and Airtran. But if Southwest expands too quickly, it risks straying too far from its original, successful formula. We've already seen how a too-rigid application of that formula deprived Southwest of its backyard opportunity at New York's JFK Airport. In the years to come, Southwest's managers will be faced with many similar stop-or-go decisions, where the correct choice will be far from obvious.

Meanwhile, JetBlue faces a similar challenge in determining the optimum speed for its own expansion. Too slow, and Southwest, ATA, Airtran, or some new player could grab the most lucrative markets. Too fast, and JetBlue could become financially overextended, which would make the company vulnerable in the event of an economic slowdown. So far, David Neeleman has been moving forward aggressively, building his jet fleet and launching service in secondary markets. Time will tell whether JetBlue's expansion strategy has been paced correctly.

HOW SOL PRICE LOST HIS MONOPOLY

Most companies that discover a new monopoly space don't have the luxury of time. If your monopoly space is attractive and surrounded by few barriers, you can't afford to wait. You *have* to fill up the entire space as fast as possible. The goal is to seize the best locations before someone else gets there. This will force the next guy to think twice about entering the same business.

An entrepreneur fortuitously named Sol Price opened the

very first warehouse club—called, inevitably, Price Club—in San Diego way back in 1976. For almost a decade, Sol was the only one in the warehouse club business—a nice little monopoly. His company grew from one location with $13 million in sales in 1977 to ten locations with $366 million in sales by 1982.

But then Sol slowed his company's growth. He preferred to stay on the West Coast and not move inland. That was a fatal mistake.

In 1981, Jim Sinegal, one of Sol's managers, left the company to start up his own discount club in Seattle. He called it Costco. Sam Walton, founder of Wal-Mart, visited Price Club and was inspired. He launched Sam's Club in Midwest City, Oklahoma, in 1983.

Sol's monopoly started eroding. By 1986, though Price Club remained the category leader, its market share had slipped to less than 40 percent. What's worse, Sam's Club and Costco were growing much, much faster. In four years, Sam's Club had opened forty-nine warehouse stores, while Costco had thirty-seven. Price Club lagged with just twenty-eight.

In 1993, Costco bought Price Club. Sol Price's monopoly was history.

Unfortunately, Sol wasn't alone in this mistake. Time and again, we see companies surrender their monopoly because they were too slow, too unfocused, or too cautious to build out far enough, fast enough.

Contrast Sol's cautious approach to that of three Seattle-based companies—Costco, Starbucks, and Microsoft. All three have been spectacularly successful thanks to their aggressive pursuit of a speed-to-space strategy.

Since its founding in 1981, Costco has been on a tear, growing from 37 locations in 1986 to 69 in 1990 to over 300 in 2004. Though less visible than Sam's Club, Costco has nearly the same number of members (42 million vs. Sam's 46 million) and generates more revenue ($34.4 billion in 2003 vs. an estimated $32.9 billion for Sam's). Costco is also more profitable. What's more, Costco has momentum, steadily, inexorably, widening the gap between itself and Sam's Club.

Then there's Starbucks. After its successful launch in Seattle, Starbucks' first intercity move was not into neighboring Portland or San Francisco (as the company's board was suggesting) but rather a huge leap into Chicago. Founder Howard Schultz wanted to ensure that Starbucks would become a national brand *from the very beginning*. Next, he jumped down the West Coast to Los Angeles, back up to San Francisco, and then clear across the country to Boston.

While initially expensive, each of these moves established the Starbucks brand in a key market that also attracted a lot of people from out of town. That was crucial, especially given that Starbucks couldn't spend much money on advertising. Each location helped transmit the Starbucks message via word of mouth into other markets. In turn, this created a buzz, a latent demand to be tapped as soon as Starbucks invaded a new area.

Microsoft is perhaps the ultimate champion at building

out fast. Once Microsoft found its monopoly—the PC-DOS operating system—they wasted no time, systematically moving into the markets for spreadsheets, word processors, e-mail, and other applications, and dominating them. They built some products themselves and bought others, including PowerPoint presentation software, the Encarta encyclopedia, and, later, Hotmail. In short, Microsoft has single-mindedly expanded throughout the ownable space in the PC software business.

DON'T RUSH TO NOWHERE!

Speed to space, then, is critical for the would-be monopoly builder. But here is a cautionary note: Don't rush to expand your business when there's reason to doubt the existence of a true monopoly space!

This is a mistake that was made by a number of companies stricken by the Internet fever of the late 1990s.

In July 1999, Internet grocer Webvan signed a $1 billion deal with Bechtel Corporation to build no fewer than twenty-six fully automated warehouses across the country. This could have been an admirable example of an aggressive speed-to-space move—except that, at that time Webvan's first and only warehouse in Oakland was operating at less than fifteen percent of capacity!

Webvan wasn't the only dot-com company obsessed with speed as a strategy. In e-tailing (Amazon, Pets.com, eToys), media (AOL, Yahoo!), e-mail (Hotmail), Internet consulting (CommerceOne, MarchFirst), or Internet software (Ariba and countless others), the idea was to grab as much space as fast as possible in order to establish "critical mass." Speed was the moving spirit of the so-called New Economy.

But speed works only when there is a real monopoly space to be seized—a space characterized by customer needs, competition that is failing to address those needs, and a new way to meet those needs profitably. Most of the dot-coms had no monopoly space. Often they didn't even have any business model, any way of generating real revenues and profits.

One of the few exceptions was eBay. Not only did the eBay auction site meet an unmet customer need in a new and profitable way, it also benefited from the network effect that is inherent in any successful auction market. The more sellers list on eBay, the more buyers flock to eBay. This causes even more sellers to list on eBay, in turn attracting even more buyers, and so on and so on. Net result: An avalanche of buyers and sellers that sweeps away everything in its path. Today, eBay is virtually the only consumer auction site left standing.

By contrast, Amazon doesn't benefit from network effects. Just because other people buy books on Amazon doesn't mean I have to buy books on Amazon. Similarly, just because one publisher sells on Amazon doesn't mean others *have* to sell on Amazon. No network effect means no natural monopoly for Amazon. But Amazon *did* create a classic *brand* monopoly, especially in books. Thanks to Amazon's aggressive (and costly) drive to establish itself as the leading Internet retailer of books, it has created a brand name that is virtually synonymous with online book sales.

So speed alone—mindless speed that isn't focused on a true monopoly opportunity—will not capture the market. But once you've found a real monopoly space and confirmed its existence through the tests we described earlier in this book, don't hesitate. Seize that space before someone else does—or forever regret the missed opportunity.

16

KEEP MOVING: MASTERING THE ART OF MONOPOLY LEAPFROG

HOP, SKIP, . . . OR *JUMP?*

Imagine you are traveling through a marshy waste that you know contains treacherous areas of quicksand. Unfortunately, it's almost impossible to distinguish the quicksand from the rest of the marsh. So long as you're standing on a patch of firm, high ground, you're safe. But you soon discover—when you pause to catch your breath only to find one foot suddenly sucked ankle-deep into the muck—that even this modest degree of safety is illusory. For at every moment, the quicksand is slowly, inexorably eroding the firm patch on which you stand. You don't dare to stay put. Instead, you have to constantly keep moving, searching for the next piece of high ground.

Welcome to today's business world.

Monopoly spaces are patches of safety in a marshland where treacherous commodity markets dominate. These isolated bits of terra firma are constantly subject to erosion as competitors nibble at the edges or grab major pieces of turf. Before you know it, the monopoly is gone and you're being sucked down into the commodity quicksand.

Long before this happens, you'd better have a new monopoly lined up, a new bit of firm ground to jump to. Otherwise, well, as the intrepid explorers who first plumbed the world's unknown desert spaces discovered, once you're sinking in quicksand, you only sink faster when you struggle.

Smart managers and companies intuitively understand this reality. Knowing that today's secure markets may be gone tomorrow, they constantly have their eyes on the next main chance.

Chastened by their earlier failure to recognize the threat posed by the Japanese invasion of the 1970s, the "big three" American automakers did a better job of anticipating danger in the mid-1980s. Recognizing that the Japanese were moving upmarket from compacts and subcompacts into full-size cars, they jumped (though belatedly) into minivans, with Chrysler in the lead. When that piece of solid ground began to crumble at the edges, they jumped into SUVs and pickup trucks, which today account for the bulk of Detroit's profits. Today they should be asking, "Where do we jump next?"

American Express has been playing a similar game of monopoly hopscotch. For decades, Amex relied on the solid footing provided by its original green charge card. When that space got crowded, they jumped to a new island—the Gold card—and then to the Platinum card. Now, with nearly every bank in the country issuing Visa or MasterCard in Platinum cards, where should Amex jump next?

Some companies have made truly radical leaps when they found their monopoly space collapsing. Nokia's original monopoly was in paper manufacturing. When that industry became commoditized, Nokia made a giant jump all the way into cellular telephones!

When it comes to mastering the art of monopoly leapfrog, timing is key. Cling to your current monopoly space too long and you could find yourself sinking in the quicksand with nowhere to jump. That's what happened to Sun Microsystems, which waited too long to jump from its Unix toehold to Linux. In the same way, Blockbuster may have lingered too long on its DVD-rental-store turf rather than making the leap to movies by mail and movies by download.

Conversely, jump too soon and you may find that the new piece of firm ground you were counting on was a mirage, an illusion—while someone else moves quickly to grab the solid space you just abandoned. So how do you know when, where, and how to make your next leap? What if you spot an attractive monopoly space while your current patch of ground is still solid? Should you stay put? Or should you jump?

REENGINEER THE FUTURE

One useful technique for mapping out the potential risks and rewards in the shifting sands of the future is known as *scenario planning*.

Entire books have been devoted to the discipline of scenario planning, but in a nutshell, it involves listing key factors likely to influence industry, competitor, and customer dynamics in the future; considering various ways in which these factors might develop and interact with one another; and then creating a handful of plausible scenarios depicting what would happen to the industry under each set of circumstances. In effect, scenario planning is the art of developing alternative stories of the future that can be used as guideposts for strategic planning.

For example, one typical scenario that the executive team at General Motors should be considering today might look like this:

Due to rising demand for energy from the developing world, along with continued unrest in the Middle East, oil prices rise to over $100 per barrel. Domestic gas prices soar past $10 a gallon. Shortly after Iran detonates its first nuclear device, the United States launches a military strike in an effort to destroy Iran's nuclear weapons facility. The attack is condemned by the Arab world, and OPEC cuts oil production quotas, leading to a new "oil shock" and long gas lines in the United States. In response, Congress introduces strict new fuel efficiency requirements for American-made SUVs, and Nissan and Honda introduce new hybrid-engine SUVs that travel sixty miles on a gallon of gas.

In this possible future environment, what should GM do?

Scenario planning is usually conducted by teams of executives representing different disciplines and points of view. You may want to invite outside experts with strong track records for anticipating future trends in demographics, economics, technology, politics, and sociology to contribute their insights. Don't get locked too quickly into the one or two scenarios you find most plausible or most attractive. Instead, spend time brainstorming freely to conjure up some of the more outlandish futures that fate may have in store. After all, ten years before the fact, very few people predicted the fall of the Soviet Union, the AIDS epidemic, the explosion of the Internet, or the horrors of September 11, 2001. Today businesses are grappling with the consequences of these once-implausible scenarios.

An alternative approach is what we might call *reverse-engineering the future*. Where scenario planning says, "These things *could* happen. What will you do about them?" in reverse-engineering, you say, "Here's what I want to do. What things *have* to happen to make this possible?"

To launch a reverse-engineering exercise, start by describing your industry and your company as you'd like them to be ten years from today. Then work backward, crafting a narrative that describes how your desired future came to be. Don't rely on implausible or unprecedented events, as in the classic S. Harris cartoon that shows a scientist developing a complex equation on a blackboard, in the middle of which appears the sentence: "At this point, a miracle occurs." Instead, try to show how the future you prefer could happen as a natural outgrowth of plausible, even likely shifts in industry, competitor, and customer dynamics, provided your firm responds appropriately.

In your reverse-engineering narrative, strive to identify

two kinds of inflection points. One is *showstoppers,* the events that absolutely *must* happen before a particular market shift occurs. The other is *trigger points,* events or changes that will start the monopoly kaleidoscope turning toward the future you imagine.

Once you've completed your reverse-engineering story, you're ready for the crucial follow-up—determining what your company needs to do, and when, to transform the future you prefer into reality.

It should go without saying that neither scenario planning nor reverse engineering offers a foolproof technique for mapping out a successful series of leaps for the years to come. The world we live in is just too complex and unpredictable for that. But one thing is certain: Standing still and hoping for the best as the landscape shifts around you is *not* a viable option.

17

WHAT TO DO WHEN THE MONOPOLY ENDS

EVERY MONOPOLY EVENTUALLY BECOMES A COMMODITY

As midnight approached on December 31, 1983, the question on the minds of many Americans was not, "Who can I grab and kiss when the New Year's ball drops?" or even, "Will I be able to get a cab to drive me home after all the champagne I've drunk?" but rather, "Will the telephones still work?"

Because everyone knew that, at midnight, the nearly century-old Bell System monopoly was due to expire. Ma Bell was being put out to pasture, her properties divided among seven regional telephone companies—the Baby Bells—and a newly shrunken AT&T.

Never before had such a large enterprise been broken up. There'd been anguish and breast-beating from unions concerned about jobs, consumers worried about service quality, and legislators trying to protect their constituents. Armies of lobbyists had descended on Capitol Hill to try to prevent the breakup or alter its terms. But the plan moved forward, and now zero hour had arrived.

Midnight came. Mercifully, America's phones still worked. But the Bell System monopoly was history. AT&T now faced competition in long-distance service, in telephone equipment, and in network equipment.

In the twenty years since then, most of the former Bell monopoly businesses have become commodities. Before the breakup, a long-distance call cost anywhere up to a dollar a minute; today it costs pennies per minute (or virtually zero over the Internet). Pay telephones were a lucrative monopoly; today almost everyone has a cell phone and phone booths everywhere are being dismantled. Telephones were expensive and had few features; today's cheap phones are loaded with features and options. You had no choice about where to buy your local and long distance service; today you have lots of choices.

What happened to Ma Bell will happen to every business someday. *Every monopoly eventually becomes a commodity.* And once a monopoly is gone, it's gone forever. The goose may still lay plain old eggs, spotless and white and wholesome to eat, but the golden eggs you enjoyed in the days of monopoly are a thing of the past.

Large government-owned or -supervised monopolies like the Bell System may break up with a huge crash. But more typically, monopolies end with very little fanfare.

Does Dell Computer still have a monopoly? For nearly a decade, Dell was pretty much the only company selling built-to-order PCs over the telephone and via the Internet.

Gradually, however, other PC makers started online stores offering much the same capabilities. Today Dell's ownable PC space is getting crowded with the likes of Apple, Gateway, H-P/Compaq, and IBM.

So where is Dell's monopoly today? Dell has been leapfrogging to extend its direct sales model into other product categories such as servers (to help businesses network their phone and computers) and consumer electronics (such as big-screen televisions), but the competition is close on its heels. So where is Dell's ownable space today? Without a monopoly, what is Dell's future?

SURVIVING COMMODITIZATION

What do you do once your monopoly is gone?

You have essentially two choices. One is to try to create a *country club* with a few rival firms fighting genteelly for market share—and with your own company in the role of industry leader. The ideal arrangement would be to split the market with only a single competitor, creating what economists call a *duopoly*. Failing that, you can settle for a small group of rivals (an *oligopoly*), none of whom spoil the fun by adopting drastic competitive measures like price-cutting. Either way, your focus is on managing the club and setting the rules.

The generic drug industry is a good example of how such clubs are created and controlled. Imagine that the drug Fixitol (which, as the name suggests, is guaranteed to fix any complaint) is nearing the end of its patent life. As the patent clock ticks, a very interesting drama starts to play out. First, the patent holder tries every means at its disposal to extend the life of the patent, including applying for new patents on Fixitol's secondary characteristics such as packaging, coloring, whatever. At the same time, generic drug makers start gearing up to produce their own versions of Fixitol for shipment on the day the patent expires. They also petition the Food and Drug Administration to dismiss the patent holder's new exclusivity claims as frivolous and unnecessary.

All this is a sideshow to the main event. In a marvelously orchestrated piece of theater, even as the patent holder and the generic drug makers are both pounding the table and shouting, "Foul!", they are quietly working hand in glove to create a nice, highly profitable little club. Here's how it works.

The patent holder knows the generic makers will price their products at between 60 percent and 70 percent off the list price of Fixitol. They also know that some 20 percent to 30 percent of drug buyers will stick to Fixitol even after generic substitutes are available. So the patent holder starts *raising* the price of Fixitol systematically for a couple of years before the patent expires. Consequently, when generics appear, they are still discounted 60 percent below the list price of Fixitol . . . but that list price is now 30 percent to 50 percent higher!

Net result: the maker of Fixitol sells fewer pills at much higher prices, while the generic makers sell lots of pills at slightly higher prices. Everyone benefits—except, of course, the consumers who use the drugs and the insurance companies that help to pay for them.

The country club approach is one way of maximizing the value of a monopoly when its days are numbered. Of course, you need to step very gingerly in creating your new club. The federal government looks askance at any actions that are overtly aimed at limiting competition, fixing prices, or otherwise controlling a market. Part of the oligopoly profits you earn will have to be earmarked to pay for top-flight antitrust attorneys to make sure you stay on the right side of the law.

The alternative approach might be called the *slash-and-burn*. As the demise of your monopoly approaches, you can begin cutting costs and prices ferociously. Your goal—to drive other competitors away from the business, keeping the bulk of the market for yourself even if, in the process, "you create a desert, and call it peace" (as the historian Tacitus said of the Roman empire-builders). Essentially, you commoditize your own products rather than wait for someone else to do it to you.

The philosophy behind the slash-and-burn approach might be summarized this way: "If someone's going to be selling this stuff at Wal-Mart prices, we might as well be the ones to do it."

That's how Becton, Dickinson and Company (BD) recaptured the market for plastic disposable syringes. BD introduced the first plastic disposable syringe in the early 1970s. Competitors soon entered the field, and shortly thereafter BD's patent monopoly ended. BD went on the offensive, building large plants and cutting costs so effectively that within a decade, it was once again the major player in the market, with Japanese entrant Terumo a distant second.

Dell is now following essentially the same strategy. Dell looks at every segment of the electronics industry and asks, "How can we enter and dominate this market by cutting costs and boosting volumes?" The strategy has proven successful in desktops, laptops, low-end servers, and networking equipment. Now Dell is trying to replicate the pattern in printers—in the process laying siege to the comfortable country club duopoly currently enjoyed by Epson and Hewlett-Packard.

The two approaches (country club and slash-and-burn) are not antithetical. You can start by creating a country club and then throw everyone out if it degenerates into "animal house." The only danger is that, once you've gotten used to the soft life of a country club, you won't have the willpower needed to throw the bums out and to cut costs and prices ruthlessly to regain market dominance.

THE WILE E. COYOTE MOMENT

Whatever you do, you mustn't allow your fading monopoly to lead you into a Wile E. Coyote moment.

You've seen it happen: Wile E. Coyote is chasing the Road Runner through the usual mountainous terrain, both of them kicking up furious streamers of dust as if jet-propelled. Suddenly, the Road Runner veers screechingly around a sharp bend in the road, and the pursuing coyote, unable to stop, careens straight ahead over the edge of a cliff. For a moment, he hovers miraculously in midair, his legs furiously pumping empty space. Then he glances down, realizes his situation, utters a feeble bleat of despair, and plummets to the canyon floor thousands of feet below.

In 1985, General Motors experienced the mother of all Wile E. Coyote moments. The once-dominant automaker had been in free fall in terms of quality and reliability since the late 1960s, while vehemently denying the existence of any real problem. When the second oil crisis hit, and the Japanese moved upmarket into full-size cars, GM's market share collapsed, dropping by ten full points—the equivalent of one million vehicles—in just two years. Imagine the shock on the face of CEO Roger Smith when he suddenly realized that he and his entire company were treading on air—and had been for more than fifteen years.

Business history tells us that the death of a monopoly, like the fall of an empire, is often inevitable, part and parcel of business evolution. It may not be fair to hold managers accountable when the inevitable occurs. But what managers *should* be blamed for is a failure to realize that their monopoly is dying and that it's time to adjust to a new set of competitive realities.

Epilogue

THE MONOPOLIES
OF TOMORROW

I want to conclude this book by returning to the New Competition and the ways in which it is revolutionizing the nature of monopoly power.

As we've seen, the emergence of the New Competition is bringing with it a series of powerful, interlocking changes. Separately and together, they are dramatically changing the business landscape.

First, customers are changing. They're growing older in the West and younger in the East. (Richie and Fonzie aren't teenagers in Milwaukee any longer—now they're grandparents in Los Angeles.) They are becoming more knowledgeable and more demanding, more fragmented and *much* less loyal to brands and companies than their parents and grandparents were in the past. In short, the single homogeneous mass market has gone the way of the nickel soda. In its place we have many market segments, each with different needs, different ways of buying, different ideals and role models, and different tastes.

Second, more people in more places know more about technology than ever before. Thanks to the Internet and other global media, they learn about new products and services almost simultaneously, which means that consumers in Beijing and Bangalore want those products and services at the same time as buyers in Toronto and Tokyo. And unlike their parents and grandparents, they are refusing to settle for yesterday's version—they want the latest and greatest, and they want it *now.*

Third, the widespread availability of technology also means that the folks in Beijing and Bangalore are able to make their own versions of the latest products faster, better, and cheaper than their counterparts in Rochester, Yokohama, Seoul, or Taipei—with or without the permission of the technology owners! Copying is easier than ever before and, thanks to the Internet and e-commerce, faster and more lucrative.

Fourth, mass merchants like Wal-Mart, Home Depot, and Best Buy, e-commerce players like Amazon.com and eBay, and hypermarkets like Carrefour are controlling ever larger segments of consumer markets in the United States and Europe. Brand and product monopolies are disappearing as these merchants use their muscle to squeeze prices (even for once-proud luxury brands) and build private labels. The growing power of the channel dominators—the "sexy beasts" of today's business—is radically changing the nature of consumer marketing.

To top it off, all these changes are occurring at a time when the entire industrial world is awash in excess capacity. From automobiles to kitchen appliances to steel to telecommunications, virtually every industry is suffering from far too much capacity chasing far too little demand. What's worse, it looks like this overcapacity is here to stay for quite some time.

This capacity glut spells trouble for asset-based monopolies built on brands, product designs and features, or unique technologies. With so much excess capacity, companies can't charge premium prices; monopoly assets don't generate the monopoly profits they once did.

Thus, in the era of the New Competition, the four traditional sources of monopoly—natural resources, regulation, collusion, and proprietary technologies—are all rapidly losing their effectiveness. Most natural resource monopolies have long been taken. Governments are *de*regulating, not handing out new, regulated monopolies. Collusion is virtually impossible, as well as illegal. And proprietary technologies are leaking away, being copied, or being replaced by newer technologies faster than ever before. The New Competition is ruthlessly squeezing the profits of the old monopolies.

Yet even as the New Competition is destroying the old monopolies, it is creating new ones. Most will be situational monopolies, naturally, since today's era of rapid, unpredictable change is generating more turns of the monopoly kaleidoscope, at a faster rate than ever before.

What's more, today's excess capacity, while it undermines traditional asset-based monopolies, makes it easier for upstart companies to tap into situational monopolies. Dell has been able to leap successfully into the markets for telecommunications equipment and consumer electronics in part because there is too much capacity and too many suppliers desperate to fill up their plants. A glut of retail space helps

Starbucks to obtain all the street corner locations it wants, and a glut of planes means that new, low-fare carriers like Southwest, JetBlue, easyJet, and Ryanair can snap up all the planes they want at the prices they want.

So where will you find the monopolies of tomorrow? If I had a precise road map, it would of course be worth a thousand times the cover price of this book. Because the future is impossible to predict, so is the location of tomorrow's monopolies. But we *can* say that tomorrow's winners—the companies that take advantage of the situational monopolies being opened up by the ever-accelerating monopoly kaleidoscope—will be the companies that are prepared to leap most nimbly from one market, one business design, and one strategic plan to the next.

In a world where change is the only constant, the worst mistake is to stand still.

Acknowledgments

This book would not have happened had it not been for Barbara Rifkind, Helen Rees, John Mahaney, Sam Hill, Karl Weber, and Blair Lele.

Barbara and Helen saw the possibilities of the idea, worked hard with me to package it right, marketed it successfully, and stayed with it through nearly four years.

John Mahaney, who also edited my earlier books, never lost his faith in me despite some trying moments and relentlessly pushed me to produce my best efforts.

Sam Hill is, in many important ways, a major off-stage collaborator and driver behind this book; in fact, it's fair to say, "No Sam, no book." A combination of spark plug and spur, Sam helped me define monopoly and give coherent shape to the monopoly rules. At crucial moments, he also spurred me to stay the course, most notably when he said, "You can either write the book or paint the house!" That did it. Thanks a million, Sam; you're a true friend and supporter.

Karl Weber came in at a crucial point and helped organize, fine-tune, and generally push the manuscript over the finish line.

My wife, Blair, read the manuscript many times and did a heroic job of copy editing for a not-always-grateful author and husband. Authors test their families severely—in time that could be available for other things, in attention or the lack of it, in moods—and Blair helped pull me through it.

Many other people gave generously of their time and

thoughts, in reading the book, in testing its ideas, and in debating with me or providing anecdotes. Thanks to:

Jack Gould, former dean, Chicago GSB, who reassured me that monopolies were quite legal and that I was on the right track.

Al Berkeley, Brian Fischer, Ken Harris, Nagesh Mhatre, and Peter Rogers, who provided me with ideas, anecdotes, and encouragement.

Bill Stowell and Jim Sharp, who graciously agreed to let me purloin their names for characters in the book.

Mike Malefakis and Steve LaCivita of the University of Chicago's Graduate School of Business, Executive Education, who were early and steadfast supporters of the book, allowing me to test various ideas through seminars all over the world.

Many participants of Chicago GSB's Executive Development Program, who provided feedback and critiques—in particular, Rob Bruinsma, Tim Fowler, George Labelle, Bob Knorr, Christopher Steane, Rob Tecco, and Scott Turner.

My colleagues Dean Chung, Jay Terwilliger, and Mark Sebell, who helped me think through how managers can identify emerging monopolies.

Index

215

About the Author

MILIND M. LELE is the managing director of SLC Consultants, Inc., a strategy consulting firm based in Chicago, Illinois. He was Adjunct Professor of Strategy and Marketing at the University of Chicago's Graduate School of Business for more than eighteen years and presently teaches in Chicago GSB's Executive Education programs all over the world. He obtained his Ph.D. from Harvard University and has published widely, including articles in *Harvard Business Review* and *Sloan Management Review* and two books, *The Customer Is Key* and *Creating Strategic Leverage*.